So Much More Than Sexy

So Much More Than Sexy

MARK ATTEBERRY

Standard®
PUBLISHING
Bringing The Word to Life

Cincinnati, Ohio

Published by Standard Publishing, Cincinnati, Ohio
www.standardpub.com

Substantive editor: Diane Stortz
Project editor: Lynn Lusby Pratt
Cover design: Susan Koski Zucker
Interior design: Edward Willis Group, Inc.

Published in association with the literary agency of Alive Communications, Inc., 7680 Goddard
Street, Suite 200, Colorado Springs, Colorado 80920, www.alivecommunications.com.

ISBN 978-0-7847-2119-3

Library of Congress Cataloging-in-Publication Data

Atteberry, Mark.
So much more than sexy / Mark Atteberry.
  p. cm.
Includes bibliographical references
ISBN 978-0-7847-2119-3 (perfect bound)
1. Christian women--Religious life. 2. Femininity--Religious aspects--Christianity. 3. Sex--Religious
aspects--Christianity. I. Title.
BV4527.A89 2009
248.8'43--dc22   2008054822

15 14 13 12 11 10 09   9 8 7 6 5 4 3 2 1

For Marilyn, Michelle, and Alyssa,

who make me so much more than happy.

Acknowledgments

Gene Fowler said, "Writing is easy. All you do is stare at a blank sheet of paper until drops of blood form on your forehead."[1] A little melodramatic perhaps. On the other hand, there are days when he doesn't seem that far off base. Because writing is so hard, you need people in your life who make it easier. I am blessed to have a lot of them. Here are a few I would be ashamed not to mention.

Marilyn, my wife, who helps me in so many ways, I couldn't begin to enumerate them. As the business aspect of my life accelerates, she keeps me organized and pointed in the right direction without ever letting any of it get in the way of our romance.

Lee Hough, my agent, who represents me with integrity and class. Long ago we moved beyond being author and agent and just became friends. We spend as much time laughing, telling stories, and sharing prayer requests as we do talking about my book projects.

Dr. Les Hardin, my friend and "Bible scholar of choice" when I need some deeper insights into a difficult passage of Scripture. He's forgotten more about the Bible than I will ever know.

Dale Reeves, Lindsay Black, Sarah Felkey, and Lynn Pratt, my friends at Standard Publishing, who are true professionals in every sense of the word . . . and fun too. They somehow plucked a concept out of my head and turned it into something you can hold in your hands.

Diane Stortz, my editor, who blew me away with her keen insights. She understood what I was aiming at in this book and helped me zero in on the target.

Kelsey Kingsbury (yes, *that* Kingsbury), who wrote the foreword. Kelsey is a beautiful young woman who epitomizes the message of this book. I am so honored that her first published words are in my book. I doubt they'll be her last.

Karen Kingsbury, a dear friend who gets the credit (or the blame) for my being a published author.

And *you, my readers,* who always inspire me with your kind e-mails.

Contents

Foreword

I grew up always performing. As a little girl I would grace-fully dance across our living room floor while loudly singing a beautiful song to Jesus. I really believed that I would grow up to become a beautiful princess, meet my perfect and handsome prince, and we would live happily ever after. And I still do. The Bible says, "'I know the plans I have for you,' declares the Lord, 'plans to prosper you and not to harm you, plans to give you hope and a future'" (Jeremiah 29:11, *NIV*). My parents gave this verse to me when I was a little girl, and I still cling to the powerful message it holds. God truly has an amazing plan for my future handsome prince and me as long as I keep my eyes toward him.

When I was a freshman in high school, I made the cheerleading team, along with all of my very best friends. I soon realized that others around me considered cheer-leaders as uneducated and simply sexy. But I desired to be an example of how a cheerleader—or any woman—really can be so much more than sexy.

Being female isn't easy. Getting ready in the morning can be a huge battle, and ladies, you know exactly what I am talking about! First we take a shower, then we attempt to blow-dry and style our hair, and last but not least is putting on makeup and choosing an outfit—and don't forget, we need to complete this mission in warp time. The time it takes a guy to get ready is no time at all (and trust me, I have five brothers!).

Women face a lot of pressure to look a certain way. We live in a celebrity-obsessed world, and we tend to look up to the stick-thin models we read about in gossip magazines. This unhealthy way of thinking is completely damaging to us personally and, in the end, to our society. I have gone through the many ups and downs of being a young woman. I've had guy problems, makeup problems, days when I felt fat, clothes problems, cravings for material things, and all of these incidents have left me feeling empty and never good enough.

Mark Atteberry's book explains the importance of beauty coming not only from the outside but most significantly from *inside*, from our hearts. (My dad has always called me his precious princess, and I think all Christian women should look at themselves as God's princesses.) While reading this book, I found that every chapter delivers an amazing truth I needed to hear. The way Mark breaks down these everyday issues of always trying to be sexy is brilliant. He gives us an inside look at a guy's brain and promises us that there are real godly guys holding out for you and me. This book is a great reminder for all women to always hold a high standard for ourselves when dealing with men, dating, marriage, and especially our self-image. God made us in his perfect image; let's cling to that truth. Whatever our age, we are *so much more than sexy*!

In God's love,
Kelsey Kingsbury
daughter of #1 inspirational fiction author Karen Kingsbury

Introduction

"*All* men think about is sex!"

You've heard it a thousand times.

If you're a woman, you've probably *said* it a thousand times.

But I'm here to tell you it isn't true. My purpose in this book is to slide a stick of dynamite under this long-held misconception and light the fuse. I think it's high time to explode this lie and let you in on a dynamic, life-changing secret: millions of men in this world are looking for so much more than sex.

Oh, I can understand why you wouldn't think so. Sadly, there are just enough classless, immature men out there to make it seem true, and pop culture constantly portrays men in the tawdriest terms possible. In the movie *Bruce Almighty*, for example, Jim Carrey plays an ordinary guy who gets to possess all the powers of God. And what does he do? Wipe out poverty? Put an end to oppression? Bring peace to the Middle East? Of course not! Instead, he sends a perfectly timed gust of wind so he can get a peek under a pretty girl's skirt. Then with the snickering glee of a hormone-crazed teenager, he has the brilliant idea of making his wife's breasts larger.

Tacky, you say?

Of course, but what do you expect? He's a guy!

Or maybe you remember the beer ad that shows two guys sitting in a crowded bar, dreaming up the perfect Miller

Lite commercial. Their naughty little minds conjure up a couple of gorgeous women who start arguing about whether the beer is better tasting or less filling. Before you can say *bimbo*, the two women are pulling hair, ripping clothes, and tumbling nearly naked into a public fountain. As the scene fades, our typical males are shown back in the bar, nodding in hearty approval, hefting their brewskies, and pronouncing their fantasy a true work of art.

Oh yes, I can understand why you would think that sex is all men care about. But speaking as a man—and one who's met and talked to thousands of other men across the country—I'm convinced there's a lie being perpetrated here. I believe that Satan, the father of lies (John 8:44), has three reasons for working overtime to hoodwink you.

First, he wants to sow seeds of disrespect toward men in the hearts of women of all ages. God has given men great leadership responsibilities in the home, the church, and the world. Therefore, anything Satan can do to make it harder for women and girls to respect men strikes a mighty blow against God's plan.

Satan also wants to sow seeds of sensuality in our culture. If he can convince you—especially when you're young—that sex is all men care about, it's inevitable that talking, acting, and dressing provocatively will seem the thing to do. And I can't think of a word that better describes our culture than *provocative*. Bare midriffs, plunging necklines, and low-riding, skin-tight jeans are the order of the day. Even preteen girls dress (and sometimes act) like the pop culture divas they idolize.

Third, Satan wants to sow seeds of hopelessness in marriages. Every time a clueless husband is preoccupied, inattentive, or rude all day long and then suddenly morphs into Prince Charming when he crawls under the covers, he unwittingly reinforces the man-as-insensitive-sex-maniac stereotype that culture has already planted in his wife's mind. She may give in to his advances, but it will likely be with a halfhearted, let's-just-hurry-up-and-get-it-over-with attitude. Pile enough of those heartless, robotic exercises on top of each other, and any woman would feel empty and hopeless.

When I started writing books several years ago, I never dreamed I'd write one for women. I'm not into Bath & Body Works, HGTV, or any of the other girlie things I see my wife and daughter enjoying. To be honest, I don't even pretend to understand women. After being married for more than thirty years, raising a daughter, and being a pastor to thousands of women, I still find them infinitely and wonderfully mysterious. I wholeheartedly agree with author Angela Thomas, who writes, "The woman is a mystery that the man can't unlock. Her desires seem to him like a moving target."[2]

But that doesn't mean I'm blind.

As a pastor I've been observing this devilish lie about men and watching it undermine God's plan for male-female relationships for a long, long time. I've finally come to the place where I have to speak up.

In this book I'm going to challenge you to reconsider some things you may have always believed about men and the best way to interact with them. No, I'm not going to try to sell you on the notion that all men are gentlemen. Clearly, many are not. But I do know without a doubt that there are still a lot of us left who can see beyond the swell of a woman's breast.

Imagine how this new understanding could profoundly change your life.

For one thing, it would take some pressure off. It would allow you to be more real, to concentrate more on the development of your inner qualities rather than always thinking you have to compete with the pretty blonde in the deep·V-neck who works in your boyfriend's or husband's office. For another, your relationship with your man could be invigorated if, instead of trying to breathe new life into your wheezing relationship with skimpy outfits and the latest perfumes, you started to build some new, more meaningful bridges from your heart to his.

If you're skeptical, I'm not surprised. I know that many women have experienced the very worst that testosterone has to offer. If you've pretty much lost all respect for men and are thinking this book is a monumental waste of paper, I plead with you to keep an open mind.

I'm not saying there's anything wrong with being sexy.

(Actually, I'm very much in favor of it!) I'm just saying that many women aim too low . . . that there's something much higher and much more wonderful for you to shoot for.

Something millions of guys would give anything to find.

Something so much more than sexy.

1

The Myths in the Mirror

Tracy, I'm in love with you, no matter what you weigh.
—Link Larkin in *Hairspray*

I wouldn't want to be a woman.

No way.

I wouldn't be able to take the pressure to always look beautiful. A guy can have a paunch, wrinkles, thinning hair, gray hair, or even no hair, and still be cast as the romantic lead in a Hollywood blockbuster, but any woman with the same physical traits will end up playing the senile grandma with an afghan over her lap, spitting out saucy one-liners between slobbers.

And this foolishness all starts at birth.

Just listen to those proud relatives pressing their noses up against the hospital nursery window. If the baby is wrapped in pink, they'll call her beautiful, gorgeous, a little doll, or a real heartbreaker one of these days. But if the baby's wrapped in blue, they'll likely predict a college scholarship for the little linebacker. I have no doubt that if you wrapped the girl baby in blue and the boy baby in pink, you'd get the same color-coded comments.

And the pressure builds from there.

It isn't long before a little girl becomes enamored with the Disney princesses, all beautifully and flawlessly rendered, and ends up shrieking with delight when her parents give her princess paraphernalia for Christmas. You can bet that even before the wrapping paper is carted away, she'll be stylin'—*click-clacking* through the house in her plastic high heels and sparkly dress, soaking up oohs and aahs from everyone except her bratty little brother, who's too busy blowing things up on his new computer game to notice.

Then of course, there's high school, where so much of the popularity pecking order is based on looks. It's the pretty girls who are the best bets to be cheerleaders, homecoming queens, and Saturday-night dates for quarterbacks and cleanup hitters.

And don't even get me started on the many doodads women use on a daily basis to ready themselves for public scrutiny. We guys only need five things in our bathrooms: a comb, a razor, a toothbrush, some toilet paper, and the sports page. We can knock off our whiskers with a dull razor, run a comb through our hair (even this is optional nowadays), brush our teeth, and we're good to go. Ten minutes tops. But you are expected to address the cosmetic needs of every feature, from head to toe.

- The hair has to be perfectly mussed.
- The eyebrows have to be plucked or waxed.
- The eyes themselves have to be lined and shadowed.
- The nose has to be powdered so it won't shine.
- The lips have to be glossed so they will.
- The ears have to have the proper bangle (or two or three) dangling from them.
- The bra has to perform miracles.
- The outfit has to coordinate.
- And the shoes have to be cute or sexy. (It

doesn't matter if they cause excruciating pain, just so they're cute or sexy.)

Finally, there's the weight issue. It's much easier to be a little overweight if you're a guy. Among other things, you'll be called strapping instead of fat (I don't know what *strapping* means, but it definitely sounds better than *fat*), you'll get to hit cleanup on the softball team, and no one will dare pick a fight with you—because heavy guys are assumed to be tough, whether they are or not.

But if you're what the fashion mags call curvy or plus size, the pressure's on . . . to buy a ThighMaster, to eat like a rabbit, to actually use your ThighMaster, to eat like a rabbit, to walk twenty miles a day, to eat like a rabbit, to sweat to the oldies, and to eat like a rabbit. If you fail to do these things with the fervor of an Olympic athlete in training, or—Heaven forbid—if you're ever seen eating a doughnut in public, someone (probably a woman who's never had a weight problem) will comment on how sad it is that you've given up or let yourself go.

Somebody, somewhere dubbed women the fair sex. I think maybe the *unfair sex* would be more appropriate because of the outrageous pressure you are under to live up to culture's current definition of beauty. I say "current definition" because the standard constantly changes.

The very first Miss America, sixteen-year-old Margaret Gorman, won her crown in 1921. I assume men back then considered Margaret to be a babe, yet any man looking at her picture today would have a hard time controlling his snickers.

In the 1950s, all eyes were on a voluptuous Marilyn Monroe. Ten years later, all the magazine covers featured a ninety-five-pound Twiggy. Fifty-year-old women were once considered way over the hill, but now women such as Michelle Pfeiffer, Oprah Winfrey, and Lauren Hutton—all over fifty—epitomize beauty, grace, and style. In fact, in 2005 *Big* magazine invited Lauren Hutton, at the age of sixty-one, to appear in its pages nude, something that would have been unthinkable a few years earlier.

No one can predict how beauty will be defined by our culture ten or twenty years from now. Who knows? Shaved heads might be the hot new trend. Absolutely nothing will surprise me. The only thing I'll bet on is that whatever culture is demanding, women will still feel pressure to try and deliver it.

Mirror Myths

Lest you misunderstand, let me say emphatically that I don't believe there's anything wrong with a woman wanting to look and feel attractive. In the musical *West Side Story*, Maria sings with exuberance about how pretty she feels. It's a joyous, refreshingly innocent moment in the story. There's no haughtiness. No panting sexuality. Just a young woman experiencing what every woman seems to long for.

"I truly believe that the longing to be known as beautiful is part of our design as women," Angela Thomas writes. "God put us together this way on purpose. We are wired to long for beauty and to be known as beautiful."[3] Nothing in my experience with women would lead me to disagree.

And yet . . . I know that what you believe when you look in the mirror can be a myth. In fact, there are three spiritually and emotionally debilitating mirror myths I'd like to explode right now.

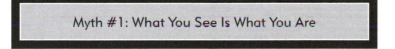

Myth #1: What You See Is What You Are

Wicked Queen Jezebel knew her days as the matriarch of Israel were numbered (2 Kings 9). Her idiot husband, Ahab, was dead, and God had chosen a young man named Jehu to replace her son Joram as king. And not only had God chosen Jehu to be king, he instructed Jehu to wipe out Jezebel and her entire family as punishment for their many sins.

Jezebel knew that Jehu and his men were coming. They had killed her sons and she was next. So what did she do? Run for her life? Assemble her bodyguards and batten down the hatches? Drink the Kool-Aid? No. "She painted her eyelids and fixed her hair and sat at a window" (v. 30).

Interesting, don't you think?

Did she get herself all dolled up in an effort to seduce Jehu and perhaps change his mind about killing her? Possibly, but I doubt it. More likely she simply thought, *If I'm going out, I'm going to go out looking good!* And keep in mind, she was the queen. She would have owned the finest garments and the most expensive jewels. When she put the finishing touches on her do and pirouetted in front of the mirror, I'm sure she was pleased with what she saw.

But she was still a hag, and everybody knew it.

A beautiful face or body doesn't make you a beautiful person, because your character is always going to trump your looks. Think about Britney Spears, once considered one of the hottest-looking females in America. There was even a TV commercial that showed a geeky, fast-food burger flipper allowing his burgers to burst into flames while he stared, open mouthed, at an overhead TV monitor where a scantily clad Britney was bumping and grinding like a cheap stripper.

But that was before her life began to unravel.

Britney's foolish choices and reckless—even brainless—behavior made her a national joke. Her endorsement contracts and public appearances dried up, not because she suddenly became physically ugly, but because her character trumped her looks.

Have you ever wondered why many of the most beautiful Hollywood actors and actresses can't stay married? You'd think if a guy was fortunate enough to marry a glamorous woman with centerfold looks . . . or if a woman snagged a hunky athlete or matinee idol, they'd never want to let go. Yet many such marriages last only a year or two and often end with much bitterness and hateful mudslinging.

Again, character trumps looks. The person hasn't been born who is gorgeous enough to overcome a corrupt heart.

Mark it down: what you see when you look in a mirror is not what you are. What's in your heart is what you are. That's why wise King Solomon did *not* say, "Above all else, make sure your eyeliner isn't smudged and there's no lipstick on your teeth." Instead, he said, "Guard your heart above all else, for it determines the course of your life" (Proverbs 4:23).

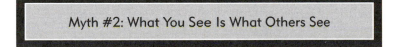

Myth #2: What You See Is What Others See

Check out these words from plastic surgeon Michelle Copeland. I found them right at the beginning of chapter 1 of her book *Change Your Looks, Change Your Life*:

> Take a long, honest look in the mirror. You can do it for real (turn on that harsh overhead light and peel off some clothing), but my bet is that you've done it often enough to know what it is about your body or face that you'd like to change.

What is it, for you? Maybe you've caught sight of that wattle that blurs your chin line (or worse, that hangs over your crisp white collar) too many times. Maybe it's the crow's-feet that grab makeup and make a spray of fright lines at the corners of your eyes. Maybe it's your nose or earlobes, both of which sag as we age. Maybe it's your "Hi Janes" (the fleshy underside of the arm that continues to wiggle after you've stopped waving hello to your friend Jane); do they make you avoid wearing your favorite sleeveless blouse or halter top? Maybe it's your breasts—how far down has gravity pulled them? Maybe it's your stomach—are you willing to expose your midriff? . . . Maybe it's your hips: Is there no A-line skirt out there that can hide hips that bear witness to every Krispy Kreme you've wolfed down? Maybe it's those pesky spider veins, crisscrossing the backs of your legs like road maps of the East Coast. I could go on and on. . . .

That's the bad news. But we're positive thinkers here, and we're going to leave harsh reality behind. Instead, let's conjure that wonderful phrase again: "What if?"[4]

This does indeed seem to be how many of you look at yourselves. You ignore the big picture (which can be very attractive) and become obsessed with the details (which are never *ever* going to be perfect). I've listened to many beautiful women put themselves down because of this or that flaw. Sometimes I've stared and thought, *Huh? What are you talking about?* I literally could not see what they believed to be so obvious.

I once heard a young woman talking about how fat she was and how she needed to go on a diet. I asked her how much she weighed (yes, she was a good friend or I wouldn't have dared), and she said, "I'm up to 120."

I shook my head. "Do you realize how ridiculous that sounds?" I asked her. "There's not another person on this planet who would call you fat." And she began to argue with me, explaining that her clothes were tight and she had flab on her rear end and the backs of her thighs.

Please get this: what you see when you look in a mirror is *not* what everyone else sees. (Unless, of course, you're the world's tallest woman, but that's another story.) Most people—guys especially—see the big picture. Yes, we are famous for checking out certain parts of the female anatomy, but that's in our God-given DNA. I still contend that most of us are not looking for or expecting perfection. We're smart enough to know that the glossy centerfold has had her pimples and moles and cellulite airbrushed into oblivion . . . and without her makeup on looks pretty much like any other woman.

I believe one of the best and healthiest things you could do for yourself would be to give up the microscopic scrutiny of every square inch of your body . . . and the whining and complaining that go along with it. I also believe God would appreciate not having to listen to you dis his handiwork. Remember, that nose you hate is a one-of-a-kind original designed by the master artist himself.

The movie version of the Tony Award–winning Broadway musical *Hairspray* released in theaters all across America in July 2007. My wife, Marilyn, loves musicals and so do I, so we were among the first to see it. We enjoyed it, but what really blew us away was how stridently it contradicts the message pop culture tries to hammer into our heads.

Set in 1962, the story focuses on Tracy Turnblad, a high school girl with big hair and even bigger dreams. She fantasizes about being one of the featured dancers on a locally produced *American Bandstand*–style television show. She also happens to think the lead dancer, Link Larkin, is the hunk to end all hunks. But alas, Tracy is considerably overweight. All the other dancers on the show are slim and trim, especially Link's girlfriend, a snooty, drop-dead gorgeous blonde who happens to be the lead dancer. Even Tracy's overweight mother (played hilariously by John Travolta) discourages her from trying out for a spot on the show, because she fears Tracy will only be humiliated. And as far as Tracy's crush on Link goes, everybody knows a good-looking guy would never be interested in a girl with a weight problem.

But two hours and several production numbers later,

the movie closes with Tracy and Link kissing center screen while snooty Miss Drop-Dead Gorgeous pouts in the background. Final score: size 16–1, size 5–0.

Unrealistic, you say?

I beg to differ.

Open your eyes and look around. The world is full of Tracy Turnblads, women who are not prototypical beauties according to society's standards but who more than make up for it with character and personality. They often end up riding into the sunset with the love of their lives, while more than a few so-called beauties in this world spend their lives bouncing from relationship to relationship and never find true happiness.

The other day Marilyn and I were in a restaurant when a family of four walked in and took a table nearby. Dad was a handsome guy, fit and clean-cut. The kids were preschoolers, cute as they could be. And mom was, well . . . let's just say she wasn't going to win the Mrs. America Pageant anytime soon. But there she sat, with a handsome husband, two cute kids, and a smile on her face.

I looked at Marilyn and said, "There sits Tracy Turnblad."

Don't think for a minute that because you aren't centerfold material you have no shot at love. It just isn't true. The next time you're in a restaurant, at a ball game, or strolling though the mall, look around at the couples. You'll see Tracy Turnblads everywhere.

Drawing the Line

This morning when I signed on to AOL, a link to seven "beauty secrets" for women appeared. With everything you've just read fresh on my mind, I had to click on it. What I found were some very interesting products. Among them:

- Control-It! Omega3 Nail Biting Cream. It's odorless, invisible, and will not stain. But it tastes bad. No way you're going to munch your pinkies with this stuff on. They say it's guaranteed to give you beautiful nails in no time. No self-discipline required.
- Fake Bake, Sunless and Skinny. The name says it all. It's a cream that promises to tan, firm, and tone you—all while you kick back and relax. Must be the seaweed it contains that does the trick.
- Poutrageous Lip Plumper. This was my favorite, "the answer to achieving the perfectly plump pout seen in all the magazines." That claim alone should guarantee millions in sales.

Knowing where to draw the line in the pursuit of beauty and romantic fulfillment is one of the biggest challenges you face as a woman. All kinds of products, treatments, and surgeries promise to work miracles on your appearance, and their suppliers will try everything they can think of (including trashing your self-esteem) to get you to fork over your hard-earned money. Let's face it. It's in their interest to keep you believing those mirror myths I just addressed. The uglier you think you are . . . the more desperate you feel . . . the more you believe your looks will determine your happiness . . . the more you feel compelled to compete with that saucy little number in the next cubicle—the better the chance they have of getting into your pocketbook.

You simply must draw a line.

No, I'm not saying your bathroom should look like a man's. I realize a girl needs her stuff. But at some point you need to slam on the brakes and say, "Enough is enough. I can be happy, feel good about myself, and have an interesting love life whether or not I achieve the perfectly plump pout seen in all the magazines."

The challenge is knowing where to draw the line.

Allow me to offer three suggestions.

Suggestion #1: Embrace Reality

Do not, under any circumstances, deny who and what you are. Not long ago MTV created a show called *I Want a Famous Face*. It featured young people who were willing to undergo plastic surgery in order to look like their favorite celebrities. Ridiculous, you say? Indeed! But before you bang the gavel and pronounce yourself innocent, realize that you can make the same mistake in nonsurgical ways.

In her book *God Chicks*, Holly Wagner talks about the time she abandoned her God-given nature in an effort to become like a couple of older women who were successful Bible teachers:

> I imitated these women in their teaching styles, their mannerisms, and their dress—all because I felt that if they were successful, then I needed to become like them. What an idiot I was!! One day as I was wrestling with my fifth pair of panty hose, and I was complaining about the sadistic man (I'm sure it was a man!) who invented them, I heard the Spirit of God laughing at me. (He does laugh, you know!) I felt that God was asking me what I was doing. I assured Him that I was getting dressed so I could go teach, and I was putting on panty hose because my two heroes wore panty hose and I needed to be like them in order to fulfill my destiny on earth. The Father quickly assured me that He didn't need me to be like them. They were fine being themselves, and He didn't need anyone else doing their jobs. He did, however, have a job for me to do on the planet, and He would empower me as soon as I was comfortable being who He created me to be.[5]

It's not unusual to see both men and women living in denial when it comes to their appearance. The guy who wears a severe comb-over or the woman who's still squeezing herself into size 8 jeans even though she hasn't actually

been a size 8 since the first Bush became president—
both are living in fantasy worlds. So is the sixty-year-old
grandma with bleached blonde hair and short shorts. So is
the teenage girl with the bare midriff who looks like she just
swallowed a football. Holly Wagner says she sensed God
laughing as she, a non-panty-hose kind of girl, wrestled her
panty hose like a python.

I can buy the notion of him chuckling at some of our
fashion misadventures, but I can't help wondering if there
comes a point where he finds it all a little heartbreaking.
When we refuse to be ourselves, aren't we saying something
about his handiwork?

I speak for a whole bunch of guys when I say that a
woman who recognizes and embraces her reality is far more
attractive than a woman who goes around every day wearing
what amounts to a Halloween costume.

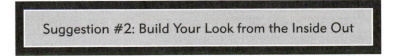

Suggestion #2: Build Your Look from the Inside Out

The apostle Peter wrote, "Don't be concerned about the
outward beauty of fancy hairstyles, expensive jewelry, or
beautiful clothes. You should clothe yourselves instead with
the beauty that comes from within, the unfading beauty of
a gentle and quiet spirit, which is so precious to God"
(1 Peter 3:3, 4). When Peter says not to be concerned about

outward beauty, I don't believe he means you should get up and go to work with bed head and bad breath. He's simply saying that true beauty flows from the inside out.

Isn't it true that people get better looking on the outside when you get to know them and realize they are beautiful on the inside? And it works in reverse too. I've met many beautiful women who, when I realized they were self-centered or immoral, suddenly started looking very ordinary.

I believe this explains how women who might be considered homely or unattractive end up having extraordinary romantic relationships. What they lack in outer beauty, they more than make up for with inner beauty. And because men are spiritual beings as well as physical, we're powerfully drawn to those beautiful inner qualities.

Sadly, even though good character is the greatest beauty secret of them all, you will probably never see it listed alongside the lip plumpers and tanning creams, online or anywhere else. Oh, and one more thing—I don't know what a six-month supply of Poutrageous Lip Plumper costs, but I know that good character is free.

Suggestion #3: Be Modest

I'll talk more about this in the next chapter, but it bears mentioning here. As you try to decide where to draw the line in your pursuit of beauty and romantic fulfillment, you're going to be tempted to believe that tighter and skimpier is sexier. Trust me when I tell you that every day we guys see women we *wish* would put more clothes on.

When I see a woman dressed immodestly, I wonder if she's trying to fill a void in her life. Is she feeling insignificant and crying out to be noticed? Is loneliness driving her to pull out all the stops in an effort to snag a companion? Do the lustful stares of strangers help her stave off the whispers of tattered self-esteem? Perhaps not in every case, but it isn't unusual for inner struggles to produce highly visible attitudes and behaviors.

The apostle Paul wrote, "I want women to be modest in their appearance. They should wear decent and appropriate clothing and not draw attention to themselves by the way they fix their hair or by wearing gold or pearls or expensive clothes. For women who claim to be devoted to God should make themselves attractive by the good things they do" (1 Timothy 2:9, 10). I once heard a woman who had just read those verses say, "It sounds like God wants us all to be frumpy." (By *frumpy* she meant matronly, unattractive, the opposite of sexy.) This is a classic example of how Satan has brainwashed us. The very notion that modesty isn't sexy has the devil's fingerprints all over it. I'm convinced that there are millions of men who actually prefer a classy, modestly dressed woman to one who looks cheap and trashy. And the men who don't aren't worth your time anyway.

Jesus said, "The world would love you as one of its own if you belonged to it, but you are no longer part of the world. I chose you to come out of the world, so it hates you" (John 15:19). This business of coming out of the world is the real issue here. It could mean different things to different people, but for a woman in our modern culture it certainly means wrestling with that image in the mirror. And wrestling might even be an understatement if you've been plugged into the world's mind-set your whole life and are just now starting to realize that God has a different plan for you. Breaking free of culture's grip and adopting a whole new way of thinking, dressing, and acting might be the biggest challenge you'll ever face. Old habits die kicking and screaming.

But they do die if someone cares enough to kill them.

And they need to die if you want to be free.

As long as you allow the myths in the mirror to dictate the way you dress, act, and feel about yourself, you will be ruling out a world of wonderful possibilities. You might feel that the more you doll yourself up, the more your horizons expand. But I believe the opposite is true. The more makeup you layer on, the shorter your hemline gets, the more risqué your conversations become, the fewer decent men will be interested in you. Oh sure, you'll grab their attention; but just remember, the monkeys at the zoo grab their attention too. That doesn't mean they want to take one home.

You have a choice. As a woman, you can work to become what culture says you ought to be or what God says you ought to be. Ultimately, your choice and your future will be determined by what you believe when you stand in front of that mirror.

So Much More Than Sexy

Do you feel anxious about your looks? Is there something (or maybe more than one thing) about your looks that you've always hated? Do you have a tendency to compare yourself to other women? What's the most radical thing (funny or serious) you've ever done to try to improve your looks?

Do you agree that character is the greatest beauty secret of them all? Can you name people who have become more beautiful in your eyes as you have gotten to know their character?

Read 1 Peter 3:3, 4. Up to this point in your life, have you worked harder on your looks or your inner qualities? What are some specific inner qualities you could cultivate that would make you more beautiful?

2

Whatever Happened to Good Taste?

Delightfully tacky, yet unrefined.
—Hooters restaurant slogan

The other day I witnessed a fight in our local supermarket. When I turned down the bread aisle, there it was right in front of me. No, not a couple of soccer moms slugging it out over the last package of English muffins. This fight was between a young woman and her jeans. And the jeans were winning.

The young woman appeared to be in her early twenties and had a small child toddling along beside her. Her jeans were at least two sizes too small and rode so low on her hips that . . . well, let's just say that when she bent over, I saw something no one but her doctor should ever see. (At least we were in the bread aisle where buns belong.)

As I watched the girl constantly tugging on her pants to pull them up, a few thoughts passed through my mind. For one thing, I wondered why she didn't just buy some jeans that fit and were tailored to be comfortable. For another, I was reminded that so many women who think they look sexy come off looking terribly silly. And finally, for the gazillionth time I wondered, *Whatever happened to good taste?*

You may be too young to remember it, but there actually was a time when movies didn't have to be rated and TV sitcoms weren't filled with sexual innuendo . . . when *Sports Illustrated* didn't have a swimsuit issue . . . when athletes weren't covered in tattoos . . . when every other newscast didn't feature a report on some inebriated, drugged-up celebrity . . . when you actually had to have some kind of talent to become famous, and love songs were really about love and not lust.

The war on good taste began in earnest in the 1960s, when I was just a boy. Theodore "The Beaver" Cleaver was too old to be cute anymore, the war in Vietnam was ticking people off, and younger Americans were growing morally restless. Suddenly, *Hair*—a rock musical featuring the use of illegal drugs, sexuality, nudity, profanity, and disrespect for the American flag—premiered on Broadway, and the game was on. Everyone seemed intent on pushing the moral envelope. John Lennon and Yoko Ono, less than a year after the premier of *Hair*, appeared nude (yes, facing the camera) on the cover of their *Two Virgins* album. Many places banned the record or sold it in plain brown wrappers, but two of the world's biggest celebrities posing like that meant all bets were off. Anything and everything suddenly seemed possible.

Today, nothing shocks or surprises us.

On her talk show, Tyra Banks was discussing plastic surgery with former *American Idol* contestant Katharine McPhee. Tyra pushed the envelope by asking Katharine if she had breast implants. When Katharine said no, Tyra picked up the envelope and tore it to shreds by asking if she could touch Katharine's breasts to verify. Katharine granted permission, and Tyra leaned over and gave her breasts a nice little squeeze. Eyes popped open and jaws dropped all across America. Tyra confirmed that Katharine was telling the truth, and I'm sure everyone who saw the show slept better that night.

During the 2007 Major League Baseball season, Alex Rodriguez of the New York Yankees put up some amazing numbers: 54 home runs, 156 RBIs, and a .314 batting average. But it was his wife, Cynthia, who grabbed the biggest headline of the season when she showed up at a Yankee home game in July wearing a T-shirt with the f-word clearly printed on the back. No, she wasn't sitting in a private box, protected from public scrutiny. She was seated in the stands, in full view of both parents and children.

Recently, Jane Fonda, while being interviewed on *Today*, used a vulgar four-letter word that refers to female genitalia. But most people barely raised an eyebrow, because just a few weeks earlier Diane Keaton had dropped her own f-bomb while being interviewed on *Good Morning America*.

Sadly, we live in a world that has lost all sense of decorum. Take the young woman in the bread aisle, for example. I don't know for sure, but I'm guessing that she threw her ill-fitting jeans into the hamper rather than the garbage can that evening. She will no doubt wear them again and again. More people will see her constantly yanking on them and will marvel at her willingness to put up with such an annoyance. A lot of guys will ogle her, and more guys than she would ever dream will marvel at her lack of taste. But through it all, she will be oblivious, because she has grown up in a culture where restaurants can be named after female body parts. She's grown up in a culture where a new celebrity sex tape lands on the Internet every other week and supposedly smart, classy women drop four-letter bombs while America eats its Cheerios. It's possible she's a nice young woman with morals far more noble than the cut of her jeans suggests. But as long as she markets her hips more aggressively than her heart, most men will never notice.

The Problem

The problem, of course, is trying to differentiate between good taste and bad taste. If both truly exist, there must be a line that separates them. But where is that line? At what point do you cross it? Or should we just conclude that all taste is in the eye of the beholder and forget it?

I agree (and I think most people do) that the eye of the beholder makes all the difference. But here's how I view that word *beholder*. As a Christian, I think it ought to be capitalized. I believe you should forget about how people (including pastors who write books!) say you should dress, and let the Scriptures teach you what is pleasing to the eye of the Beholder. Have you ever thought about what that would be?

In chapter 1 we looked at 1 Timothy 2:9, where Paul said, "I want women to be modest in their appearance. They should wear decent and appropriate clothing and not draw attention to themselves by the way they fix their hair or by wearing gold or pearls or expensive clothes."

A verse like that ought to provide us with a breakthrough on this subject. Those words *modest*, *decent*, and *appropriate* seem like they ought to solve our problem, but they don't. I can illustrate the reason why with a story.

I grew up very sheltered in a small, southern Illinois town of a thousand people, so you can imagine the culture shock I experienced when I moved to St. Louis to go to college. I'll never forget the first time I went with a carload of upperclassmen to see the Cardinals play. It was after 10:00 PM when the game ended, and as we all piled into the car, the driver asked if we wanted to "go down Washington Street" on the way back to the campus. I had no idea what that meant, but everyone else was up for it, so I said, "Sure."

Boy, was I in for a big surprise.

In those days, Washington Street in St. Louis was what some people called Hooker Heaven. Prostitutes stood along the curb every forty or fifty feet, displaying themselves for the rowdy males passing by in a bumper-to-bumper parade of cars traveling about five miles an hour. There was a lot of rude banter between the girls and the passersby, and I assume they struck some business deals along the way. I learned later that the sellers had to be very judicious because some of the buyers were invariably undercover cops.

(By the way, if you're wondering how a group of Bible college boys even knew about Hooker Heaven, I was too.

It turns out there was an inner city mission in the area, and a couple of the upperclassmen I was with had put in many hours of volunteer work there. They had a heart for street people and, through the mission, had found opportunities to witness to several of the prostitutes.)

But the thing that made the biggest impression on this small-town hick was the gaudy, tasteless, almost comical way the women dressed. I'd never seen anything like it. It was as if the worst costume designer in Hollywood history had outfitted them all for roles in a low-budget sexploitation flick. The shorts were cut high, the halter tops were cut low, and the lipstick was so red it almost glowed in the dark. I've never seen as many bleached blondes in one place. Drop any of those women into the suburbs and she would have stuck out like a seven-footer in a room full of toddlers.

What's heartbreaking is that now, more than three decades later, I see young women eating in restaurants, going to the movies, and shopping at the mall who are sporting similar fashions. Perhaps not as cartoonish, but just as short, just as tight, and showing just as much skin. No, these girls are not prostitutes. Some of them might even be Christians. I'm sure most of them don't see themselves as doing anything wrong. But anyone my age sees the change that has taken place as women's (and girls') fashions have become strikingly sexual. And I'm not the only one who thinks so. Author and counselor Grace Dove says that prostitutes have not started dressing more like regular women; regular women have started dressing more like prostitutes.[6] As a result, whatever line once existed between decency and indecency has been all but erased.

And that's the problem with 1 Timothy 2:9. Our culture has beaten the words *modest*, *decent*, and *appropriate* and left them for dead by the side of the road. If you're an average young woman, they don't even register on your radar screen. If you're the mother of a teenage girl, you've probably discovered that any attempt to discuss those words is met with a lot of eye rolling and head shaking. Yet I still think 1 Timothy 2:9 offers us our best hope of finding God's will on this matter. The key is to do a little digging.

The Original Sex Symbol

Look at the verse again: "I want women to be modest in their appearance. They should wear decent and appropriate clothing and not draw attention to themselves by the way they fix their hair or by wearing gold or pearls or expensive clothes." And verse 10 adds, "For women who claim to be devoted to God should make themselves attractive by the good things they do."

It's critical to understand that Paul made this statement in a letter to Timothy, a young preacher living in Ephesus, the capital of the Roman province of Asia. Timothy faced many challenges there, not the least of which was trying to establish a church in the shadow of the temple of Artemis, one of the seven wonders of the ancient world. Four times larger than the Parthenon, the temple stood 390 feet long, 210 feet wide, and 6 stories high, majestically framed with 127 pillars, each 6 feet thick and 60 feet high.[7] Artemis, also known as Diana, was the goddess of fertility. If you ever see a picture of the cult image crafted to depict her, you'll notice she has braided hair, what seems to be jewelry, and many breasts hanging all over the front of her body. (Talk about subtle!) We call good-looking movie stars or celebrities sex symbols, but there's never been a more obvious symbol of sex than Artemis.

Naturally, you're wondering how people worshiped such a goddess. Well, think about it. If a God of holiness and love is pleased when we offer him holiness and love, then what do you suppose would please a goddess of sex? Scholars tell us that the prostitutes who "served" in the temple wore short skirts and left one breast uncovered.[8] Simply put, the place was pulsing with sexuality. Picture Bourbon Street during Mardi Gras. Imagine craftsmen making and selling little statues of the many-breasted Artemis (see Acts 19:23-27) the way Disney sells Mickey Mouse souvenirs. The worship of Artemis made Ephesus famous for sensuality the way Las Vegas is famous for gambling.

And it was to the Christian women of that city that Paul wrote 1 Timothy 2:9, 10, which I believe should shape the way we think about what he said. He wasn't being a stuffy old geezer when he challenged them to dress modestly and decently. He wasn't against women looking pretty or attractive—he simply wanted them to be *distinctive*, to *not* look like the women involved in the thriving, sexualized cult worship Ephesus was famous for.

Taken in its historical context, this verse suddenly becomes a lot easier to interpret. Instead of having an eye-rolling, generational quarrel over the words *modest*, *decent*, and *appropriate*, you realize that your duty as a Christian woman is simply to have a distinctive appearance. In other words, whatever the hot, sexy babes of the world are wearing, you should be wearing something else.

Righteous, Yet Reasonable

The challenge is to be righteous, yet reasonable in your dress. You want to put forth a good witness without dressing like the Queen of England. You want to find that happy place somewhere between a nun's habit and a hooker's garb. Let me offer some righteous, yet reasonable ideas.

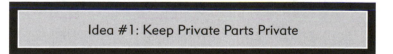

Idea #1: Keep Private Parts Private

Trust me when I tell you that the guys who are dying to see your midriff and your cleavage are the same guys who are going to go home and scroll through porn sites on the Internet. When you see them gawking at you and salivating, you might get a small thrill. Your self-esteem might momentarily be buoyed. But understand, to them you are a piece of meat. In their fantasies you will not have a face or a heart or a personality. When you dress in such a way as to hold nothing back, you lose two ways: the good guys don't want you and the bad guys only see you as an object.

Author Leslie Ludy drills the truth dead center when she encourages women to try to recapture the art of feminine mystique:

> Mystique means guarding what is sacred, protecting the essence of who we are from the inside out—our hearts, emotions, intimate thoughts, and physical bodies. A woman with mystique preserves the treasure of who she is, keeping herself set apart for the one who proves he is worthy of such a gift. Feminine mystique is a lost art. Today it is far more vogue to hold nothing sacred than it is to protect our hearts, emotions, or bodies. It is even considered prudish or snobby to hold purity sacred and fool yourself into believing that there actually is a man out there somewhere who will value your heart as a treasure.[9]

Trust me. There *is* a man out there somewhere who will value your heart as a treasure. And I want to tell you something about that man: he doesn't want to see your body parts right now. He knows you have them and that they aren't going anywhere. When and if the time is ever right, he'll be interested. Very interested. But until then, he wants to know what makes you tick. He'd like to learn about your hopes and dreams. He'd like to hear the sound of your laugh and get an idea of what tickles your funny bone. He'd like to know if you have a temper and what triggers it. He'd like to find out what frightens you. He'd like to know if you're tenderhearted and forgiving and if you're impatient, a procrastinator, or a neat freak. In other words, he wants to burrow down into your heart and find out what you're hiding in there. What's more, he understands that it's fun and exciting to dig for and discover hidden treasures—much more fun and exciting than cheap sex that's over in a flash and has no future.

So keep your private parts private. Don't contribute to the objectification of women everywhere by giving the perverts of this world one more faceless body to drool over. Instead, be mysterious! Leave something to the imagination. And if some guy shows interest, make him earn his access to your heart. The ones worth having will be happy to do just that.

Idea #2: When You Go Shopping, Take Your Faith with You

One time I ran into a young woman at a department store. Because we are friends, the natural thing would have been to stop and chat for a moment, but she obviously felt awkward and couldn't get away from me fast enough. And I knew why. She was wearing a top that left almost nothing to the imagination. In fact, it reminded me of the famous P. G. Wodehouse quote, "She looked as if she had been poured into her clothes and had forgotten to say 'when.'"[10] I could tell she felt embarrassed, not only by her stammering and her red face but also because during the brief time we did talk, she held her purse in an unnatural fashion to cover her cleavage.

I felt sorry for her. It's terrible to be embarrassed. But I wondered, *Girl, what were you thinking when you bought that top?* Probably price, color, brand name, fabric, and how "cute" it was. But the one thing she apparently wasn't thinking about was how it would impact her Christian witness.

Dear sister, if you want to live the spirit of 1 Timothy 2:9, 10 . . . if you want to be recognizable as a Christ follower in a world that's lost its mind over sex, you simply must take your faith with you when you go clothes shopping. You can't just buy whatever hot new fashion the window mannequin happens to be wearing. You've got to think about how that article of clothing will shape the conclusions people draw about you. Don't ask yourself if you would be embarrassed to be wearing it if you happened to run into your pastor. Ask yourself how you'd feel if Jesus saw you wearing it . . . because he will!

You might also need to go through your closet and get rid of some things. If you've been buying indiscriminately for some time, you probably have quite a few articles of clothing that need to be discarded. But don't sell them on eBay or drop them off at Goodwill or the Salvation Army so someone else can grab them and make the same mistake you've been making. If the clothes are inappropriate for you, they're inappropriate, period. Just throw them away.

Idea #3: Don't Send Mixed Signals

My friend Arron Chambers describes an aspect of his childhood you might relate to: "When I was growing up, I had 'church clothes'—the ones I was allowed to wear only on Sundays. I was not permitted to play in them. If I wanted to play, I had to put on my 'play clothes.' If this was not confusing enough, I also had 'school clothes.' Apparently, they could help me learn in a way my play clothes could not because I was never allowed to wear play clothes to school."[11]

As adults we continue to have different clothes for different occasions. If we set different standards of taste for those different kinds of clothes, however, we end up sending mixed signals.

Several years ago I accidentally attended an anniversary

party for a well-known jazz radio station in Orlando. A friend and I literally walked through the wrong door and found ourselves in the middle of a crowd of mingling VIPs in tuxedos and party dresses. We were dressed in Dockers and polos and were just about to turn around and leave, when a smooth jazz band kicked off its set on the far side of the room. That did it. We decided to stay and listen until security threw us out. They never did, and while we were there I had an interesting experience.

I saw one of the local TV news anchors, a beautiful woman my wife and I had watched for years. I was used to seeing her in her professional, conservative work clothes, but on that night she was obviously wearing her "play clothes": the legendary, quintessential little black dress (with *little* being the operative word). A decent seamstress wouldn't have needed much more than a couple of good-size dinner napkins to duplicate the thing. I'd like to tell you I didn't stare. I'd like to tell you I immediately looked away and started quoting Scripture to keep my mind pure. I'd like to tell you I immediately called my wife and told her I loved her. I'd like to tell you all of these things, but I can't. The truth is, I did stare, if only for a moment . . . after I picked my eyeballs up off the floor and stuck them back in my head. And I wasn't the only one.

Please don't misunderstand.

I'm not condemning that news anchor. My point is simply that, as a Christian woman, you mustn't be like worldly women who have one set of standards for their public or professional lives and a much lower set for their private or "playtime" lives. In fact, it's when you find yourself in a secular environment that your spiritual mettle is really tested. Paul's admonition to "come out from among unbelievers, and separate yourselves from them" (2 Corinthians 6:17) doesn't even kick in until you find yourself surrounded by worldly people with standards much lower than your own.

Remember, you are God's child whether you are at church or at the company Christmas party. You need to bear the family resemblance wherever you go.

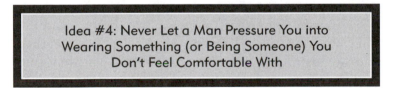

Idea #4: Never Let a Man Pressure You into Wearing Something (or Being Someone) You Don't Feel Comfortable With

At the beginning of the book of Esther, we find the story of King Xerxes of Persia (a hero to Scrabble players everywhere) and his wife, Vashti, one of the gutsiest women in the Bible. Unfortunately, Xerxes was a lousy husband. One day while at his palace in Susa (just north of what is now the Persian Gulf), the original X-Man threw a party for his servants and officials. It lasted seven days and there was only one rule: each man could drink as little or as much booze as he wanted.

I'm sure I don't have to tell you that the king and his

cronies were feeling no pain by the end of the week. In fact, the Bible says Xerxes was indeed tipsy when he ordered Vashti to be brought out so the other drunks could ogle her. Vashti responded (translated from the original language), "No way, José." She flat-out refused, which ticked off the king and placed him squarely in the throes of a dilemma. If the queen could get away with defying the king, said the royal advisers, then women throughout the kingdom might start feeling their oats and refusing their husbands' demands, which, of course, would never do. So the king banished Vashti and sent a letter throughout the kingdom, proclaiming that every man should be the ruler of his home.

Sadly, though King Xerxes has been dead for millennia, his spirit lives on in certain men. Perhaps you are dating or married to a dumb oaf who cares nothing about your feelings but insists that you wear things or do things you don't feel comfortable with. And maybe you do it because you think it's your duty. Or maybe you've never dated a decent guy and you think all relationships work this way, or the newness has worn off your marriage and you think you have to do it to keep him interested. Trust me. It's *not* your duty, all relationships *don't* work this way, and if you have to cheapen yourself to keep him interested, he's probably already got his eye on some other hot little number anyway.

If this insensitive, classless Romeo is your boyfriend, you probably need to dump him. If he's your husband, find a good counselor who can help you set up some boundaries. Either way, you simply must refuse to be pressured into dressing or acting in ways that compromise your convictions. The cold, hard truth is that you might indeed suffer the same fate as Vashti if you draw a line in the sand; your man might banish you and go looking for a replacement. If that happens, your next move should be to buy some ice cream, get out the party hats, and celebrate your liberation, because you, my friend, are going to be much better off.

Always remember: it's better to be banished by the "king" than by the King.

~~~~~~~

Universal Studios in Orlando has an event every fall called Halloween Horror Nights, advertised with pictures of grotesque monsters on billboards all over the city. Disney World, just a few miles down the interstate from Universal, has a not-so-scary Halloween party with Mickey Mouse and his friends. Disney, too, uses billboards to advertise, but there are no pictures of scary monsters— just Mickey, Minnie, Donald, Daisy, and Goofy wearing innocent, childlike Halloween costumes.

I can look at those billboards and know exactly what each park is selling and what kind of clientele it's going to attract.

Your body could be compared to a billboard. You put

something on it every day that tells the world what you're selling. If you dress in skimpy tops and tight jeans that ride low on your hips, or if you go braless or wear T-shirts with suggestive sayings on them, don't be surprised when a guy who's in the market for sex wants to do business with you. Don't be surprised when he approaches you with rude or sexual comments. Hayley DiMarco is right when she says to women, "We can't get mad at guys for being guys. We can't blame them for following us down the path of objectification when that's the package we've put together."[12]

Starting today, think of yourself as your own marketing agent. Identify exactly what it is you're selling. Picture the kind of "clientele" you want to do business with. And then dress accordingly.

So Much More Than Sexy

Do you have any articles of clothing that you wear because you think they look good, even though they are annoying and uncomfortable? Do you have clothes you would be embarrassed to be wearing if you bumped into your pastor? Have you ever bought and worn clothing you didn't feel comfortable with just to try to please a man?

In your opinion, what is feminine mystique? Based on your definition, how hard have you tried to develop or maintain it? Have you ever lost a relationship with a guy you liked, simply because you were determined to hold some things back? How did that make you feel?

Does your closet reflect obedience to 1 Timothy 2:9? "I want women to be modest in their appearance. They should wear decent and appropriate clothing and not draw attention to themselves by the way they fix their hair or by wearing gold or pearls or expensive clothes." If you are the mother of a teenage daughter, do you find yourself battling with her over her wardrobe? What can you share with her from this chapter to help her evaluate her closet and understand the importance of modesty?

3

Brains vs. Breasts

Why do I need a brain as long as I have these?
—Abercrombie & Fitch T-shirt

We're taught as children that we have private parts. Society firmly insists that male private parts remain private forever, but with women it's different. At some point it's permissible for some of your private parts to go public. Research has shown that a girl with cleavage will enjoy undeniable advantages over her flat-chested sisters.

This explains a couple of things.

First, it explains why the bra is the most engineered of human garments, boasting thousands of patents, and why there are around eight hundred new bra designs hitting the market every year. This becomes an astounding number when you realize that it takes fifty people in seven departments working over six months to lock in the design of one new bra.[13] We know that a dog is man's best friend, but author Eve Marx says, "A great bra is a girl's best friend. No article of clothing can do so much for you."[14] Countless women obviously agree.

Second, the "need" for cleavage explains the phenomenal growth of the cosmetic breast-augmentation business. For some women, even the most miraculous of miracle bras won't cut the mustard, so surgery becomes the answer. Implant surgery is the second most common plastic surgery procedure (behind liposuction), and coming on strong.[15] There has been a 64 percent increase in breast-augmentation surgery since 2000, and even though the Food and Drug Administration recommends that a woman be eighteen before having the surgery, an alarming number of underage girls (3,500 in 2005) are having it.[16]

The fact that breast augmentation is expensive (usually over four thousand dollars) is no hindrance at all. These days even a single mom earning minimum wage can get her implants for free. All she has to do is sign up with a certain Web site that connects females who have flat chests with males who have fat wallets. If the woman agrees to provide him with pictures and videos of herself (before and after, but *especially* after), he will make a donation to her cause or, if he *really* likes the videos, pay for the entire procedure. As I write these words, the site is boasting 1,100 happy testimonials and another 1,000 "members" looking for donations.

What's ironic is that in such a breast-obsessed culture, a nursing mother has to retreat to a private area or cover herself with a baby blanket if her child needs to suckle while she's at the mall, a restaurant, or the airport. I guess the moral of the story is that men love your breasts as long as you're not using them in a way God intended. You can inflate them, tattoo them, lift them, scrunch them together, and flaunt them to beat the band and it's cool, but if you dare to let us see you using them to sustain life, you're in trouble.

The temptation, of course, is to blame men for this insanity, and I don't deny that we bear considerable guilt. On the other hand, I don't exactly see an Amazonian mind-set in women either. The Amazons were mythical female warriors who lived apart from men except for one visit a year for the sole purpose of creating pregnancies. When the babies were born, the Amazons nurtured the girls and killed the boys. But they are most famous for their self-inflicted mastectomies. They are said to have cut off one breast to improve their archery skills so they could keep the surrounding male hordes at bay.[17]

No one's denying that men can be pigs, but there always seems to be a crowd of women around the pigpen. For example, I'm writing these words during spring break, which for most of us who live in Florida is a complete annoyance. Last night, in between political updates, Fox News carried a report on the Girls Gone Wild phenomenon (which I'll discuss in chapter 4). Cameras at Daytona Beach showed giggly college girls baring their breasts, not just on the beach but on street corners, in gift shops, in restaurants, and anywhere else someone happened to dare them. Another clip showed a wet T-shirt contest in which the participants were judged after a pitcher of ice-cold water was poured over their chests. (Imagine the media frenzy we'll see someday if one of those girls runs for public office and some enterprising cameraman with a good memory produces the video.)

But it's not just creepy pornographers and tipsy college girls who contribute to the *breastification* of America. Not long ago, a Christian mom I know opted to have her breasts enlarged. Curious (and with this book brewing in my head), I asked her why. She said it had nothing to do with any desire to attract men. She said she was doing it for herself and no one else. Nice answer, but it doesn't explain why, after the surgery, her neckline took a plunge that made the stock market crash of 1929 look like a minor hiccup.

Don't get me wrong. I'm not saying that in order to be a good Christian you have to bind and smash your breasts like the flappers of the 1920s. That would be just another form of denial. I'm simply saying once again that in a sexually charged, breast-obsessed, life-is-one-big-spring-break culture, you as a Christ follower need to be different. And by different, I mean special. Any female with an IQ to match her shoe size can raise her top and giggle. It takes a special woman to realize she has something far more interesting to offer.

The Other B Word

A short distance north of your breasts is your brain (the other *B* word). It weighs approximately three pounds (relatively close to the same weight of the average pair of breasts) and represents about 2 percent of your body mass. It's not pretty to look at. They don't make lingerie for it. You'll never see one gracing the cover of *Playboy* or *Maxim*. But make no mistake: your brain greatly influences how attractive you are to the man worth having.

Oh sure, the Neanderthal type doesn't care if you have the intelligence of a slug as long as you'll sleep with him, and the intellectual wimp is intimidated by any female smarter than he is. But the guys worth having in this world are fascinated by and drawn to brainy women.

Maureen Dowd is a Pulitzer Prize–winning columnist for the *New York Times*. She is witty, articulate, and liberal. I don't agree with much of what she writes, but I couldn't resist when I saw her book *Are Men Necessary?* I checked it out of the library and hauled it home, thoroughly curious but expecting to be ticked off before I completed the introduction. I was, yet I also found a few things in the book that affirmed some of my long-held beliefs.

For example, at one point Dowd shares some e-mails she has received from men who are attracted to brainy women. A young man from Toronto wrote: "For months I have been sullenly wondering if there are any women out there who have IQs that actually exceed their body temperature. What would I do to meet a woman who treats her head as more than just a frilly decorative ornament!"

Ms. Dowd also includes this humorous testimonial from another man:

> Shortly after we were married, my wife tearfully confessed that her IQ, at 178, was 45 points higher than mine, that she had been the salutatorian of her college class and was a member of Phi Beta Kappa. I was shocked, but divorce was out of the question. It has been terrible to live with, but there have been compensations: 1) Our children are a lot smarter.

2) She remembers people's names, places we have visited, and learns foreign languages the way I catch colds. Men, don't fear that cute little genius you have your eye on.[18]

It takes a while, but the man worth having eventually realizes that life is *not* one big spring break. In the course of time, it dawns on him that all women have breasts but the real treasures are the women who also have brains. He can be a very slow learner. Blinded by the sloshing hormones of youth, he sometimes doesn't come to this realization until he's already married, which I'm convinced explains a high percentage of divorces. But there does indeed come a time when being married to a girl whose major accomplishment in life is being a former wet T-shirt champion no longer makes him feel like a lottery winner.

Here's the sobering truth: your body will attract a guy, but it won't keep him very long. For one thing, there are too many other great bodies out there. No matter how good yours is, you don't have to sit for more than two minutes on a bench at your local mall before some girl with a body just as good comes sauntering by. The saying "There are other fish in the ocean" has its roots in this eternal truth.

Also, guys don't sit around and think about sex constantly; we dismantled this deception in chapter 2. If they did, you might be able to hang onto one with a few good push-up bras and a couple of tube tops. But since the guys worth having are interested in other things too, you will find the need to have a conversation once in a while. If you can't do it intelligently . . . if you can't spar with him, inspire him, even wow him once in a while with an insightful observation, he's eventually going to get bored, and nothing Victoria's Secret sells will be able to reel him back in.

Face it. A good guy falls for and sticks with a woman who has some depth. There's nothing he loves more than to be attracted to a woman he thinks is beautiful, only to discover there's even more to her than he could see. That's one of the most exciting moments in any man's life. On the other hand, one of the most disappointing moments in a man's life is when he's attracted to a woman he thinks is gorgeous, only to discover there's much *less* to her than he had hoped.

Brain Augmentation: The Benefits

Because I'm a man, I can't claim to understand all the pressures you feel with regard to looks in general and your breasts in particular. I know those pressures must be incredible. As I was doing research for this chapter, I watched a BBC documentary entitled *My Small Breasts and I*. It featured several women, all of whom I thought were very attractive, who agonized over the size of their breasts. One young woman who appeared to be in her twenties said, "I feel boobs are a natural birthright and that I missed out. I feel grotesque having a flat chest." I'm confident that no one else on the planet would consider her grotesque. In fact, I suspect many women would envy her slender figure and pretty face. Yet I know her feelings are real, and I wouldn't dare minimize them.

But there is one thing I know beyond any doubt: it's never a mistake to augment your brain. We can debate the pros and cons of expanding your bust size, but there's no question that an expanded mind makes for a better life. When looks are all you have to offer, they are all you will be judged on. But when you have depth, men can look right past the size of your breasts and still find plenty to be drawn to. Sounds good, doesn't it?

An Augmented Brain Makes You Much More Interesting

My wife, Marilyn, and I still laugh about what I call the most boring evening of my life. Before I tell you what happened, you have to understand that I am no tool guy. At a recent church workday, as I was weed eating around the building with a power trimmer, I noticed that a young woman kept walking by very slowly. Every time I looked up, there she was, staring at me. I checked my fly. I made sure some wise guy hadn't stuck a silly sign on my back. Finally, I shut the trimmer down and asked her what she was doing. She said, "Somebody saw you with that machine in your hands and told me to keep an eye on you because you'd probably end up hurting yourself."

That's me and tools. Not exactly a match made in Heaven.

Anyway, when my wife and I were young, we were invited to another couple's house for dinner. We didn't know them very well, but they seemed nice, so we accepted the invitation. When we were finished eating, the women started clearing the dishes, and our host invited me out to his workshop to look at his tools. The only tool I was interested in seeing was a dessert fork, but I manufactured a smile and followed him out to his shop like Tim "The Tool Man" Taylor himself.

An hour later, my host was still talking. I had done nothing but nod and say, "Oh really?" as he showed me every tool he owned and told me where he got them, how much they cost, and how some of them worked. All I wanted to know was which one would enable me to kill myself with the least amount of pain. When we left that evening, I told Marilyn that our marriage depended on her not accepting more of that couple's dinner invitations.

Some women can talk only about soap operas or shopping or the latest celebrity tabloid headlines. Being a one-dimensional thinker makes anyone boring, period. And getting breast implants or a nose job won't suddenly make *you* interesting; it will simply give the men you're talking to something a little more interesting to look at while they're dying their slow death. On the other hand, multidimensional women who can converse intelligently on a variety of topics are generally fun to be around.

An Augmented Brain Makes You More Capable

Many years ago I attended a John Maxwell conference at a time when I was feeling overwhelmed and discouraged with my ministry. Something I learned at that conference transformed my life and ministry.

Maxwell helped me realize I was making a classic mistake: I was spending 80 percent of my time and energy on high-maintenance people who were probably never going to change anyway. I was begging them, placating them, counseling them, humoring them, and bending over backwards to make them happy . . . and had almost nothing but fatigue and frustration to show for it. No wonder I was depressed. What I needed to do was give that group 20 percent of my time and start investing the 80 percent in the people who were eager and hungry and burning up to make a difference. I couldn't wait to get home and start making that adjustment in my weekly routine. When I did, things instantly started getting better. My passion revived and my energy was renewed because I could see results. I was no longer the hamster on a treadmill.

This is an example of how just a slight augmentation of your brain—one little thought or idea plugged in and applied—can make a huge difference in your capability. Imagine how your life could change if you corralled a dozen good ideas and started putting them into practice!

An Augmented Brain Makes You More Prudent

Not long ago I stumbled across a very depressing book that consisted entirely of the confessions of people with deep regrets. This entry, from a young woman named Jennifer, was typical:

> When I was twenty-six, I met someone I had admired for years: a rock star. He had a reputation for being a real ladies' man, and a lot of people warned me about getting involved with him. But I didn't listen because I thought we had sparks, magic—something—and I was sure I would be the woman to end his roving ways. We dated for about eight months and then he flatly dumped me for an exotic dancer. I was devastated. I was so in love with him, but I was merely another conquest for him.[19]

The key words in that sad confession are "A lot of people warned me. . . . But I didn't listen." It's one thing to be blindsided by tragedy, but when you had every opportunity to see it galloping toward you like a runaway stallion and you still missed it, that's the ultimate heartbreak. Yet this is the common fate of women who lack discernment. Proverbs 27:12 says, "A prudent person foresees danger and takes precautions. The simpleton goes blindly on and suffers the consequences."

We tend to dislike cut-and-dried characterizations.

We always feel more comfortable when there's a little wiggle room in the middle. But as is often the case in the book of Proverbs, this verse boldly slices all of humanity into two groups: prudent people and simpletons. Prudent people tend to live happy, successful lives while simpletons tend to play starring roles in courtrooms and on newscasts. The good news is that you can move from the latter group to the former by augmenting your brain.

Brain Augmentation: The Procedure

I have good news and bad news.

The good news is that brain augmentation is not a surgical procedure.

The bad news is that brain augmentation is not a surgical procedure.

On one hand, it would be nice if you could be put to sleep and wake up with an augmented brain. Overnight you could be more interesting, more capable, and more prudent. On the other hand, surgery is always risky business. As I write these words, the big item in the news is the death of Stephanie Kuleba, an eighteen-year-old high school senior from Boca Raton, Florida, who was headed to medical school. She died of complications from breast surgery that was supposed to be routine. And not only is surgery risky, a study published in the *Annals of Plastic Surgery* indicates that women who have their breasts enlarged run a higher risk of suicide.[20]

Brain augmentation is a nonsurgical procedure. It is, in fact, an adventure that happens over time as the brain owner steps out of her range of thought and experience and starts exploring a world that's full of wonder. If you want to undertake this adventure and better yourself, here are four action steps.

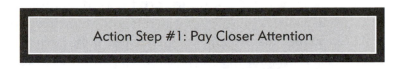

Action Step #1: Pay Closer Attention

Significant, enlightening things happen all around you every day. People you may or may not know speak important words and do both good and bad things—all with the potential to be valuable life lessons—but most of us sail through life on autopilot and completely miss them. We look, but don't see. We hear, but don't listen. We assume instead of checking to make sure. D. Q. McInerny, a former professor of logic at Notre Dame, says, "The phrase 'to pay attention' is telling. It reminds us that attention costs something. Attention demands an active, energetic response to every situation, to the persons, places, and things that make up the situation. It is impossible to be truly attentive and passive at the same time."[21]

Here are three areas of your life where paying attention might really pay off.

First, pay attention to why people suffer. For example, if you have a friend who's going through a hard time, ask yourself why. It could be that she did nothing to cause it (and that in itself is a life lesson). But if she made a mistake, you immediately know what not to do.

Second, pay attention to why people succeed. If you're struggling with your marriage, pay attention to couples who have great marriages. If you want to be a better mom, pay attention to moms who are raising great kids. If you want to get your finances in order, pay attention to women who make less money than you do but aren't up to their eyeballs in debt. If you feel hopeless or pessimistic, pay attention to people who have a song in their heart and a spring in their step. Some of the greatest lessons I've ever learned have come just from watching people who *were* what I wanted to be.

Finally, pay attention to new ideas. A new idea is any idea that's new to you, even if it's been around for thousands of years. Why new ideas? Because they challenge and stretch you, and that's what brain augmentation is all about. Not all new ideas are good ideas, but you will never know if you slam and lock the door of your mind to them all.

Action Step #2: Read More

James Allen, an Englishman who lived more than a century and a half ago, wrote that the mind "may be likened to a garden, which may be intelligently cultivated or allowed to run wild; but whether cultivated or neglected, it must, and will, bring forth. If no useful seeds are put into it, then an abundance of useless weed seeds will fall therein, and will continue to produce their kind."[22]

Reading is the best and most enjoyable way to put useful seeds into the garden of your mind.

I often tell people that I got my PhD at the Salvation Army store. They think I'm kidding, but I'm not. For years I've gone to the local thrift store one day a week, usually on my lunch break, to look through the books. I almost never walk out empty-handed. I've bought novels, biographies, commentaries, leadership books, history books, sports books, health books, reference books, self-help books, and even joke books, all for pennies on the dollar. I won't tell you that I read every word of every book. Some books resemble some people: they look great but bore you half to death. For that reason, I give up on quite a few books and donate them right back to the store. But over the years this little routine of mine has augmented my brain like you can't believe.

Reading has improved my communication skills by making me a better speller and writer. It's empowered me to accomplish things that were once out of my reach. Books have sparked my imagination by carrying me away to distant times and lands. They've challenged my thinking and forced me to embrace new ideas. They've helped me appreciate people who are different from me. They've advised me, motivated me, corrected me, calmed me, and fired me up. I wouldn't be an author today if I hadn't fallen in love with books.

Unfortunately, most people don't feel the way I do about books. I was flabbergasted to read recently that 59 percent of Americans don't own a single book. Not a cookbook or even the Bible.[23] Is it any wonder there are so many uninteresting, incapable, imprudent people in the world? Imagine how you could thrust yourself to the front of the line by becoming a reader of good books.

If you're not a reader, but would like to try to become one, may I offer some suggestions?

First, choose your books the same way you choose your friends. There are some friends you're better off not having and some books you're better off not reading—and for the very same reasons. I don't care if it's number one on all the best-seller lists. I don't care if Oprah recommended it. I don't care if everyone's talking about it. If the content isn't helping you in some way, chuck it. Remember, the whole idea is to plant *useful* seeds in the garden of your mind.

Second, don't read a book if you're not enjoying it. Not every book is good, and some good books won't interest you. Nothing kills the desire to read faster than a boring book. I generally give a book fifty pages to grab me. If it doesn't, I toss it aside and move on to something else. With so many wonderful books out there, life is too short to read a snoozer.

Third, take your book with you wherever you go. You never know when you're going to get a few unexpected minutes of available time. I've read thousands of pages while sitting in the drive-through line at the bank, on a bench at the mall while my wife tries on a pair of shoes, in doctor's office waiting rooms, and in restaurants as I wait for my food to be served. Marilyn and I seldom walk out of the house without our books.

And finally, think *cheap* and *free*. It will be expensive if you buy all your books new, but by visiting your local thrift store and the library, you can read great books for very little or for free.

Action Step #3: Change the Channel

TV can be a good influence in your life or a bad one. The key is how you push the buttons on your remote. If you watch sex-drenched music videos, cheesy soap operas, mindless sitcoms full of juvenile bathroom humor, or ridiculously overhyped reality shows (which are about as far from reality as you can get), you will burrow yourself deeper and deeper into the sludge of our morally bankrupt culture. You can do that if you want to, but we're talking brain augmentation here. Watching trash TV will make you a clone of the tens of millions of others who are, for all practical purposes, brain dead.

In Philippians 4:8 Paul said, "Fix your thoughts on what

is true, and honorable, and right, and pure, and lovely, and admirable. Think about things that are excellent and worthy of praise." If you were really going to live by that verse, how many of your favorite shows would you have to quit watching? No, I'm not suggesting that you sit around and watch programs you have no interest in simply because they're educational. Entertainment is fine, but there's good, thought-provoking entertainment and then there's mush.

Explore the news channels too, and find one you like. You might know the names of Brad Pitt and Angelina Jolie's children or all the *American Idol* winners in chronological order, but don't expect the man worth having to be swept off his feet if that's all you can talk about over dinner.

Action Step #4: Take a Class

Is there a subject you've always been interested in or a skill you've always wanted to learn? Is there a training program or seminar that might help you get a promotion or a better job than the one you currently have? If so, then why not go for it? You'll not only be a more marketable employee, you'll also add to your depth as a person. Taking a class isn't as difficult as it used to be, because so many classes are offered online.

John Miller wrote the book *QBQ! The Question Behind the Question*. I was looking over the table of contents one day and saw a chapter entitled "We Buy Too Many Books." I thought those sounded like fighting words, so I found the page and started reading, with my blood already beginning to boil. But I quickly calmed down. Though I chafe at the idea that there's such a thing as buying too many books, I knew his point was a good one: "We attend too many seminars. We take too many classes. We buy too many books. We play too many audios in our cars. It's all wasted if we're unclear on what learning really is: Learning is not attending, listening, or reading. Nor is it merely gaining knowledge. Learning is really about translating *knowing* what to do into *doing* what we know. It's about changing."[24]

He's right. All of the action steps I've mentioned will be a monumental waste of time if you don't find a way to apply what goes into your head. The whole point of brain augmentation is not to enlarge your hat size but to deepen your life, to make yourself more interesting, more capable, and more prudent—to blow right on past sexy and become something so much more: intriguing.

And you can do it all without a scalpel ever touching your skin.

So Much More Than Sexy

Have you had, or been tempted to have, elective breast-augmentation surgery? Is there some specific incident or conviction that triggered this desire? Do you know anyone who's had the surgery and regretted it? Do you know anyone who's had the surgery and seen her life dramatically transformed for the better as a result?

The importance of physical attraction is a given in romantic relationships, but have you lived as if it is as important, more important, or less important than mental and spiritual attraction? Have you ever broken up with a guy you thought was really good-looking, simply because there was nothing beneath the surface? Could you be happy in a long-term relationship with someone intellectually shallow?

Romans 12:2 says, "Don't copy the behavior and customs of this world, but let God transform you into a new person by changing the way you think." If life transformation happens between the ears, what are you currently doing to facilitate it? Can you name something you need to learn or a skill you need to develop that would significantly add depth to your life? What specifically can you do to move in that direction?

4

Girls Gone Mild

When you bring your baby girl home from the hospital, will you hope with all your heart that she grows up to be a stripper?
—Kathleen Parker

If you were eating a sandwich at McDonald's and saw Joe Francis walk in, you wouldn't look twice. He is the quintessential average Joe. He could be the guy who works in the paint department at Home Depot or does window tinting at the local flea market on Saturday afternoons. He does *not* look like what he is: a big-time pornographer. Fresh out of college and armed with a business degree, our boy Joe decided to try to make the world a better place. No, he didn't build a homeless shelter, start a preschool, or run for public office. Instead, he established a franchise called Girls Gone Wild.

GGW has a pretty simple business model. Joe and his buddies arm themselves with video cameras and venture into party-hearty areas like beach communities and college towns. They hang out at Mardi Gras, slip into frat parties, and barhop during spring break, constantly inviting young women to bare their breasts, buttocks, and genitals for the camera. Then they splice those clips together, slap a suggestive title on them, and sell them for as little as $9.95.

Naturally, you're wondering what Joe has to offer the girls in return for their cooperation. Fifty bucks? A hundred? Two hundred?

Try again.

He offers them a GGW T-shirt.

I'd love to tell you that very few young women respond. I'd love to tell you that Joe's compiled only enough footage for a couple of videos. But just the opposite is true. As I write this, Girls Gone Wild has eighty-two videos circulating. GGW's problem is not getting young women to expose themselves; the problem is sifting through all the girls who want to, picking the sexiest ones, getting them to sign releases, and making sure they're not underage.

So how does a girl reach the place where she's willing to trade her dignity for a T-shirt?

Alcohol is one answer, of course. Many of the GGW "starlets" fall somewhere between tipsy and stone-cold drunk at the time of their filming. But surely, no woman would ever humiliate, devalue, and objectify herself in this way unless her internal moral compass had stopped working properly. And you don't just suddenly wake up one morning with a malfunctioning moral compass. You don't go from teaching Sunday school one day to flashing your breasts in a bar the next. The road from little-girl innocence to GGW headliner is a dark and descending one, but it must look attractive on the front end. Otherwise, Joe Francis wouldn't own a nine-million dollar jet and a silver Ferrari.[25]

Clearly, that front-end attractiveness is the lure of this thing we call sexy. To be called a babe, to be thought of as hot, to be flirted with and stared at and envied is the most important thing in the world to many young women. It means popularity, privilege, and often money, and it rules out the possibility of ever having to endure a lonely Saturday night. The problem is that chasing sexy can take you farther than you ever planned to go. There truly is a kind of hysteria that can swallow you up, a torrent that can carry you away to unthinkable places. And when you get there, guys like Joe Francis are waiting with leering smiles and mini cams.

Girls Gone Mild

What I pray for is a movement of a different kind to sweep across the country. We could call it Girls Gone Mild. How refreshing it would be to see a generation of young women rise up with internal moral compasses functioning with the accuracy of a finely tuned Swiss watch. How cool it would be to see godly give sexy a run for its money!

I'm not speaking just for myself, remember. I keep telling you that Joe Francis has a lot of polar opposites out there—decent, godly guys (who don't have tape on their glasses or wear pocket protectors and high-water pants) who couldn't watch one of Joe's videos without weeping. Though many in the feminist movement undoubtedly disagree, I contend that the *slutification* of American females upsets as many men as it delights, and probably more. I've heard it said that Joe Francis is a typical guy doing what every guy would love to do if he only had the courage. That's nonsense.

But let's get back to Girls Gone Mild.

Every new movement needs a manifesto of sorts, so let me offer one here and now: ten reasons why godly beats sexy coming and going.

Reason #1: Godly Has a Future; Sexy Doesn't

Second Peter 3:11 says so: "Since everything around us is going to be destroyed . . . , what holy and godly lives you should live." See it there in the first part of the verse? Everything around us is going to burn up and melt away (vv. 10, 12). That includes every Girls Gone Wild video ever made, along with Joe Francis's college diploma, mini cam, private jet, and silver Ferrari.

Think about it.

The daily, diligent pursuit of sexy requires a commitment to things with no future. If you live to chase sexy—even if you never end up in a GGW video—you still end up focusing on things that will mean nothing when you stand before God. Trust me. At that moment, he's not going to ask what shade of lipstick you use or who does your hair. Imagine the horror of standing before God and having nothing to show for your time on earth except a cute outfit you found on sale at the Gap.

Oh sure, being sexy gets a lot of "pub" now. I'm reminded of that every time I push my cart through the checkout line at our local supermarket. The fashion and gossip magazines always feature the latest, greatest hottie. But make no mistake: sexy's days are numbered. (Yours are too if you live to make sexy your god.)

Reason #2: Godly Can Be Defined and Measured; Sexy Can't

One of the problems with trying to be sexy is that we can never really pin it down. What's attractive to one person is disgusting to another. Tattoos are a good example; so are the various celebrities the media fawns over. Julia Roberts, for instance, is generally considered to be a sexy woman, but I look at her and think, *Huh? Are you serious?* Or perhaps you've seen a couple who looked mismatched. Maybe you looked at the woman and thought, *I wonder what he sees in her!*

This, of course, can be very frustrating for the person who's chasing sexy. If you grow your hair long because your boyfriend thinks it's sexy but then he dumps you, do you then get it cut just in case the next guy you have your eye on might not like long hair? And what about the color? Is that saying about blondes having more fun really true?

The beautiful thing about godly is that you *can* pin it down. You never have to wonder if you're on the right track. For example, the word *godly* appears sixty-four times in the book of Proverbs alone. That book, as well as any other, captures the essence of godliness. Among other things, it tells us:

    ⚖ The godly are directed by their honesty (11:5).

- The plans of the godly are just (12:5).
- The godly acknowledge guilt and seek reconciliation (14:9).
- The godly think before speaking (15:28).
- The godly love to give (21:26).

I could go on, but you get the idea. There's nothing mysterious about godliness. It is clearly defined and measurable. You never have to wonder how you're doing. Simply compare your life to Scripture and you'll have your answer.

Reason #3: Godly Can Always Grow; Sexy Eventually Slips Away

Occasionally AOL puts a link on its homepage that says something like this: "See '60s TV star at 87." I sometimes click on one of those links. For one thing, I grew up in the '60s, so I'm curious to see who it is. But the pictures I find are good reminders that sexy is the ficklest of friends. I won't mention any names, but a couple of my childhood TV sweethearts have become almost unrecognizable. And I'm sure that if an old girlfriend who hasn't seen me in thirty years saw me today, she'd probably shake her head in pity and breathe a sigh of relief that she dumped me when she did.

Proverbs 21:21 says, "Whoever pursues righteousness and unfailing love will find life, righteousness, and honor."

Righteousness is another word for *godliness.* The key word in this verse is *pursues.* Sexy is something you catch (maybe) but then lose. Godly is something you pursue throughout your life. No matter how much you acquire, there's always more to get.

Another point that should be made here is that it's never too late to start pursuing godly. People have come to Christ in their eighties and nineties and only then started the pursuit. But there is a point at which any pursuit of sexiness is about as silly as asking Rush Limbaugh to chair the Democratic National Committee.

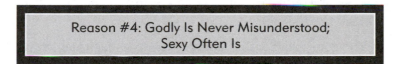

Reason #4: Godly Is Never Misunderstood; Sexy Often Is

Consider these insightful words from syndicated columnist Kathleen Parker:

> It's little wonder boys and young men are confused by constantly shifting and conflicting signals about how they should behave toward the lovelier sex. Torpedoed by cultural messages that are relentlessly sexual, by pole-dancing moms and prostitots decked in baby hookerware, they are nonetheless expected to treat females as ladies. Except, don't call them "ladies," which is insultingly patriarchal. Depending on a woman's mood, a male is expected to know exactly when to respond to her wiles by issuing a devastating

compliment; or when to pretend he hasn't so much as noticed her strategically plunging décolletage. Above all, he must be sensitive to her vulnerabilities—except when she's feeling empowered. The deal is basically this, fellas: Females can flaunt their foliage when, where, and how they choose, and you males have to be psychics to respond appropriately.[26]

I applaud Ms. Parker for saying so well what many women never seem to think about. I suspect the number of men who've gotten their heads bitten off or who've been charged with harassment for saying something about sex to a woman who's obviously gone out of her way to try to look sexy would favorably compare to the population of China.

The good news is that godly is easily understood. Never will a godly person bite your head off or accuse you of harassment for saying something about God.

Reason #5: Godly Relieves Stress; Sexy Feeds It

Women who are in hot pursuit of sexy have a lot on their minds. They're constantly wrestling with troublesome questions.

- Does this outfit make me look fat?
- Does that weight-loss pill really work?

- How can I get rid of these stretch marks?
- Would I look better as a blonde or a brunette?
- How long will it take me to save up for that surgery?
- If I put these shoes on my VISA, will I still be able to make my minimum payment?
- What does he see in her? What does she have that I don't have?

When you walk into a butterfly house, the little guys are everywhere, fluttering all around you. If you stand still, they'll land on your head, shoulders, arms, and legs. Now imagine that butterfly house as the brain of a woman who's chasing sexy, and all those butterflies as anxious, worrisome thoughts.

But if godly is your goal, it's like somebody opened the door and let the butterflies escape. There's just so much a godly person doesn't have to fret about. The Bible calls this peace. Philippians 4:7 says, "His peace will guard your hearts and minds as you live in Christ Jesus."

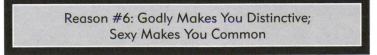

Reason #6: Godly Makes You Distinctive; Sexy Makes You Common

Women in an all-out pursuit of sexy never seem to recognize this great irony: they're practically turning backflips in an effort to be noticed, but the more they sexy themselves up, the more they look like everyone else.

Do you remember the music video of *Simply Irresistible* by Robert Palmer? All those leggy brunettes in the background look so much alike that if you squint your eyes a little, you'd swear they're all the same person. Doesn't that pretty much describe young women today? Look around when you're at the mall. Take a good look at those high school girls gathered at the bus stop. It's like the attack of the clones!

As Christians we would do well to remember what the prophet Jeremiah said: "What is the chaff to the wheat?" (Jeremiah 23:28, *NKJV*). Chaff is the outer, throwaway covering of seeds of grain. God must be heartbroken when one of his daughters chooses to join the hordes and present herself to the world as if she were chaff. I also believe the truly decent guys in this world are ultimately on a search for the heart of the grain—the wheat. Imagine the tragedy when a really good guy sees a really good-hearted girl but misjudges her because, from a distance, she looks like common chaff.

Reason #7: Godly Builds Confidence; Sexy Feeds Insecurity

This too is a great irony: young women sold out to being sexy look so self-confident as they flaunt the merchandise, strutting like supermodels at a photo shoot—but many of these girls have terrible insecurity problems. I know because I've counseled them. I've listened to them talk about their weight problems, eating disorders, loneliness, complexions, and of course, boyfriend problems. I don't know who coined the term *drama queen*, but it perfectly describes the young woman whose whole world revolves around her appearance and popularity. She always lives on the edge of panic because one little glitch in the cosmos (like a zit on her nose or a rip in her tights) is all it takes to send her universe spinning out of control.

But godly girls are different. They have an air of confidence about them, for two reasons. One, they grasp what's important. They understand that so much of what worldly women worry over is silly and inconsequential in the grand scheme of things. Two, they know they have an ally in God. Proverbs 28:1 says, "The wicked run away when no one is chasing them, but the godly are as bold as lions." It's easier to be confident when you know God is by your side.

Reason #8: Godly Propels; Sexy Limits

Isaiah 58:8 is an intriguing verse. God is speaking to his people when he says, "Your godliness will lead you forward, and the glory of the LORD will protect you from behind." I've found that godliness does indeed lead people forward. In fact, the world is full of people who can joyously testify that their lives were going nowhere until they found God and established a real, growing relationship with him. I contend that many of the world's greatest leaders and achievers have been people of great faith.

On the other hand, think about people who have made sexy their god.

Someone like Paris Hilton comes to mind. Her whole existence seems wrapped up in looking as sexy as possible and mugging for the paparazzi. Her three greatest accomplishments are a CD that was the joke of the music world, an underground sex tape, and a jail sentence. Some résumé, huh?

Anna Nicole Smith is another example. When she died, the media was all Anna, all the time. With so much ballyhooing going on, you would have thought she was the First Lady. But was hers a forward-moving life?

It's not just Paris and Anna Nicole. Try to think of even one girl gone wild who is also making a truly significant and worthwhile contribution to humanity.

Reason #9: Godly Lowers Risk; Sexy Raises It

In one sense every woman who chases sexy walks a tightrope. She lives in a world populated by people driven by their baser instincts. The spirit of seduction hangs in the air like a fog. Though not everyone in that world is dangerous, plenty of takers and exploiters are on the prowl, always leering at her, beckoning her, offering her whatever they think it will take to get her to step over the line.

Hey babe, want a T-shirt?

Even godly people are tempted and make mistakes in a fallen world, but not as often. Proverbs 11:6 says, "The godliness of good people rescues them." It rescues them from all kinds of pain and heartache simply by keeping them out of harm's way. When you pursue godly, it takes you in a totally different direction. In real terms, it's the difference between putting on your hottest outfit and going to a singles bar or taking in a concert in the park with your best friend. It's the difference between trolling sexy chat rooms on the Internet or curling up on the couch with a good book. The places you go, the people you hang out with, and the things you do for fun are all much safer.

Reason #10: Godly Is Sexy to the Godly

Are you reading this chapter and agreeing with me, yet feeling a little sad? If you're assuming that to become a Girl Gone Mild means giving up any dream of ever being thought of as sexy by a handsome man, take heart! The beautiful, often-forgotten truth about godliness is that it is extremely attractive to men who also have a heart for God.

Remember, many men will never be captured by sexy alone. No matter how hot you are, they'll be wary of you until they begin to see that you have some spiritual substance. Unlike some other men, they'll be trying to see *beyond* your bustline to the heart that beats behind it.

Right now you may be screaming, "Mark, where *are* all these godly guys you're talking about? I've been looking for a man who would look beyond my bustline for years and have never been able to find one!"

Let me be clear about something. I'm not suggesting that godliness is the *only* factor involved in attracting a great man. In fact, two people could both be very godly and still be awful as a couple.

Dr. Neil Clark Warren, founder of eHarmony and universally recognized relationship expert, says there are fifty different similarities that help to make a great relationship.[27] The more of them you have, the better your chances of making a great life together. But the mystery of how people find each other and how those similarities connect is still just that—a mystery. If you want to explore it, there are other books you should read. All I'm saying is that godly is very attractive to a man who has a heart for God.

The Essence of the Girl Gone Mild

To close this chapter, I want to tell you an obscure Bible story that illustrates the importance of putting God first and saying no to the pressures of the world.

First, a little background.

In 2005 I released a book entitled *Walking with God on the Road You Never Wanted to Travel* (Thomas Nelson), based on the Israelites' forty-year sojourn through the wilderness. To prepare, I spent an entire year reading and rereading the books of Exodus, Leviticus, Numbers, and Deuteronomy. Those books came alive to me as never before, and I found things in them that—while there all along—had somehow escaped my notice in the past.

Like the story of Shiphrah and Puah.

They were Israelite (Hebrew) midwives instructed by the new king of Egypt to kill all the Israelite boy babies as they were being born. The king, you see, thought the Israelites—slaves in Egypt—were becoming too numerous. He was afraid they might someday rebel and take over his country. And since he wasn't keen on the wholesale slaughter of adults and children, he figured the next best thing was to have the midwives twist the neck of every little boy baby as he came out of the womb. The idea was to make the boy babies look like stillbirths.

But Shiphrah and Puah would have none of it. Exodus

1:17 says, "Because the midwives feared God, they refused to obey the king's orders. They allowed the boys to live."

This, of course, didn't sit well with the king. So he called the two midwives in and asked them why they weren't obeying him. Boy oh boy, I would love to tell you that they stood up to him and said, "Sorry, buster, God is our boss, not you." But they didn't. I hate to say this, but they lied. They said, "The Hebrew women are not like the Egyptian women. . . . They are more vigorous and have their babies so quickly that we cannot get there in time" (v. 19).

I can't believe the king bought such a goofy answer, but I suspect he also believed his kids when they told him the dog ate their homework. So I'm thinking, *Ladies, maybe you were able to fool a dumb ol' king, but you just got yourselves in trouble with God. He is NOT going to be happy with you. Don't you know he hates lying?* But the very next verses say, "So God was good to the midwives, and the Israelites continued to multiply, growing more and more powerful. And because the midwives feared God, he gave them families of their own" (vv. 20, 21).

I don't pretend to always know the mind of God, but I think the message here comes through loud and clear. When you turn your back on the pressures of the world and do what you know God would want you to do—even if you don't get it all quite right—God will bless you. He's not looking for perfection; he's looking for a heart with an obvious bent toward his will.

That's the essence of the Girl Gone Mild.

She isn't perfect, but she senses when culture demands something of her that would disappoint God, and she somehow finds the courage to say, "No, I won't go there. I won't do that."

Jeremiah 6:16 says, "Ask for the old, godly way, and walk in it."

That's my challenge to you.

You may never run into Joe Francis or his team of camera-wielding perverts. You may never be asked to expose yourself in return for a six-dollar T-shirt. But you *will* face the temptation to make little compromises. Sexy will come at you from every direction and tell you that you need to lighten up, loosen up, and let your guard down.

Don't listen.

Instead, ask for the old, godly way, and walk in it.

So Much More Than Sexy

What do you think has to happen (or not happen) in a young woman's life to make her go wild or trade her dignity for a T-shirt? If you went through a wild stage and came out of it, what precipitated that change of course? Some people think it's good for young people to "sow some wild oats" and get it out of their systems. Do you agree? Why?

Have you ever felt unsexy because you were trying to live a godly life? Have you ever been secretly envious of the wild female who seems to be having so much fun? As you pursue godliness, do you think most people see you as being weird or special? Have you ever been attracted to a guy primarily because he was godly?

Jeremiah 6:16 says, "Ask for the old, godly way, and walk in it." What can you point to in your own life that represents "the old, godly way"? Like Shiphrah and Puah, can you point to some pressure you've resisted simply because of your desire to maintain a commitment to godliness? Is there something going on in your life right now that stands between you and a serious commitment to God?

5

Sugar and Spice, My Foot

In the sex war, thoughtlessness is the weapon of the male,
vindictiveness of the female.

—Cyril Connolly

I'm sure you've heard it said that little boys are made of "snakes and snails and puppy dog tails" while little girls are made of "sugar and spice and everything nice." I don't mean to trigger another skirmish in the long-running battle of the sexes, but I don't agree. I've known more nice women than I could count, but it's also true that most of the meanest people I've had to deal with have been female.

I've been in the ministry for well over half my life and have served five different churches. I recently made a list of the ten most difficult church members I encountered in all that time, and eight of them were women. (I even ran the list past my wife, and she agreed that I picked the right people.) I can also tell you that most of the conflicts I've mediated over the years have been between women or sparked by a woman.

If there's one thing I've learned working with people, it's that women take a backseat to no one when it comes to a good scrap. There's no fight like a catfight, no shoulder quite as cold as the one belonging to an angry woman, and no tongue quite as sharp. I've seen 250-pound men who stormed beachheads cower in fear of their wives. Why do you think "Hell hath no fury like a woman scorned" has become such a time-honored saying?

I've noticed that most of this testiness is triggered by and directed toward other women. Not all of it, of course. We guys have found a myriad of ways to get on your nerves. But research shows that you reserve your heavy artillery for one another.

Sugar and spice, my foot.

Susan Shapiro Barash wrote a book about female rivalry called *Tripping the Prom Queen*. She interviewed five hundred women from a wide range of ages, classes, ethnicities, and religions, asking them directly about their experiences with other females. The results of her research are telling.

- Women who indicated that envy and jealousy toward other women color their lives: 90 percent.
- The number who said they have encountered jealousy in other females since grade school: 80 percent.
- The number who reported that competition in the workplace occurs primarily between women rather than between women and men: 90 percent.
- More than 65 percent admitted to being jealous of their best friend or sister.
- More than 70 percent said they were familiar with the concept of stealing a friend's husband, lover, boyfriend, or job.
- Of those same women, 40 percent reported themselves victims of another woman's theft of a husband, lover, boyfriend, or job.
- And 25 percent admitted that they themselves had stolen a friend's husband, lover, boyfriend, or job.[28]

Popular culture reflects what those numbers indicate. Movies like *Heathers*, *13 Going on 30*, *Hairspray*, *Mean*

Girls, and even the kids' classic *Cinderella* play up the girls-hating-girls angle. Reality shows like *The Apprentice*, *Survivor*, *The Bachelor*, *Big Brother*, and *Real World* give us a ringside seat to some of the nastiest catfights you'd ever want to see. Even sitcoms aren't exempt. Do you remember the *Seinfeld* episode where George Costanza's high school gym teacher mistreats him by, among other things, giving him a wedgie and calling him George Can't Stand Ya? After hearing George relate these embarrassing incidents, an appalled Jerry looks at Elaine and says, "Girls don't do anything like that, do they?"

She responds, "Oh no. We just tease each other until one of us develops an eating disorder."

Internet entrepreneurs are also aware that females aren't all sugar and spice, and have found ways to profit from the flying fur. For example, Sissyfight is an online game that describes itself as "an intense war between a bunch of girls who are all out to ruin each other's popularity and self-esteem." As a player, you are encouraged to "majorly dis your opponents and mess with their faces and crush their self-esteem until everybody knows they are mega-loser sissies." The Sissyfight Web site claims that the game is "a lot like life."[29]

Don't be deceived by all the pop culture trappings however. This is not a new problem. Catty females have been scratching and clawing at each other for a long, long time. The term *cat* to describe a spiteful, backbiting woman can be traced back to the 1600s.[30] Further back, in the Bible,

Sarah and Hagar treated each other with contempt (Genesis 16:4-6), the sisters Leah and Rachel locked horns in a jealous feud (Genesis 30:1-22), two prostitutes fought over who was the mother of a single baby (1 Kings 3:16-28), and Euodia and Syntyche squabbled so intensely that Paul heard about it while in prison and mentioned it in his letter to their home church (Philippians 4:2).

But the Bible's Most Catty Female Award has to go to Peninnah. She and Hannah were married to Elkanah. First Samuel 1:6, 7 says, "Peninnah would taunt Hannah and make fun of her because the LORD had kept her from having children. Year after year it was the same—Peninnah would taunt Hannah as they went to the Tabernacle. Each time, Hannah would be reduced to tears and would not even eat." In that culture, where a woman's primary job was to provide heirs, being childless was a crushing humiliation. Penninah must have had a heart as black as the nighttime sky to find such pleasure in being so mean.

As I was preparing this chapter, I asked my wife for her thoughts on the untoward behavior of the so-called fair sex. She said she could remember girls mistreating other girls as far back as the third grade. Annie Chapman, in her book *Smart Women Keep It Simple,* shares a letter one little girl wrote to another:

> Dear Ramona,
> How are you? I am fine.
> Would you like to be best friends? I like you better

than I like Holly. I do not like Holly at all anymore. Let's not like Holly together.

Your best friend,
Kate[31]

Imagine those two in high school when they suddenly realize they've got a crush on the same boy!

A Time to Reflect

You might be thinking, *I ought to skip this chapter because what he's saying here doesn't apply to me.* Could be. The world is full of nice women, and you might well be one of them. But before you make that assumption, consider this: most catty women don't usually see themselves as being difficult; they often see everyone else as being slow or lazy or incompetent or stubborn and themselves as being God's answer to the problem. And it's amazing what petty problems can bring out the claws and fangs.

I'll never forget the time two women stood face-to-face in our church kitchen, arguing over a bottle of ketchup. (That's right, a bottle of ketchup.) One of the women had purchased supplies (including said ketchup bottle) for an event one of our ministry teams was planning. But before the event happened, the other woman, who didn't even know about that event, was cooking burgers and dogs for a youth group party and grabbed the ketchup out of the fridge.

The way those two women were going at each other, I

doubt that Hulk Hogan would have had the courage to step between them. Fingers pointed, veins bulged, and worst of all, spectators gathered. Had I known this flap was coming, we could have sold tickets and made some money. But since we didn't, the best course of action seemed to be intervention. We pulled the women into a side room, shut the door, and had a long talk. They both calmed down, eventually apologized, and walked out feeling pretty ashamed.

I tell you this story to show that sometimes people don't see themselves the way they really are. Maybe you're one who does. But then again, maybe you're one of the many who don't.

To be on the safe side, take a moment to do some reflecting. Think through these statements that I offer with a little tip of the cap to Jeff Foxworthy. You might be a catty woman if the following apply to you:

- You have a hot temper.
- You're outspoken by nature.
- You've been fired more than once.
- You've been engaged more than once.
- You've been married more than once.
- You're exhilarated by a good argument.
- You consider yourself a good debater.
- You've been told that you should have been a lawyer.
- You always have to have the last word.
- You think your ideas are usually better than everyone else's.

- Your best friend today isn't the same person it was a year ago.
- Your best friend a year ago wasn't who it was a year before that.
- You routinely send your food back to the kitchen when you eat out.
- You have a hard time forgiving.
- You frequently say *idiot* and *stupid*.
- You feel most people have it easier than you do.
- Your social calendar is wide open . . . and has been for quite some time.

If only a couple of those statements apply to you, I wouldn't worry too much. But if a half dozen or more hit home, there's a good chance you're more catty than you realize. Not only that, but you've probably done some damage along the way, whether you meant to or not.

A Time to Repent

When you decide to pursue godly rather than sexy, as we talked about in chapter 4, how you think about yourself and how you dress aren't the only areas of your life you need to evaluate. Your disposition is also critical. There are few things more unattractive to men and disappointing to God than a jealous, hateful, competitive, catty female. If any of these adjectives could describe you, it's time to make a change. It's time to repent.

Repentance is a word that indicates making a U-turn. To repent is to do an about-face, to move in a completely opposite direction. That's why in the Bible we find it tied to conversion. People who wanted to be saved were told to repent (Acts 2:38) because *coming* to Christ means *leaving* the world.

But repentance is not a once-and-for-all-time event. As saved people, we need to keep repenting throughout our lives as we realize our thoughts or actions are displeasing to the Lord. Right now, if you're seeing yourself in this chapter, you need to repent. You need to do an about-face and start living up to that sugar-and-spice reputation. God does not want you, his precious daughter, to be known as a catty woman. It doesn't help you at all (and it certainly doesn't help him).

But radical change is hard. If you're in your thirties or forties (or even older) and you've been combative from day one, that's a lot of history to overcome. Your contrariness is no doubt very ingrained. That's why you probably won't be successful if you try to change through sheer willpower. Willpower tends to wilt under pressure. That's why so many New Year's resolutions never live to see Groundhog Day. You have the best of intentions, get all fired up, and put on your game face. You buckle your chin strap and put a little strut in your walk. Yes sir, you're going to give that ol' devil what for. But a month later, you're often right back where you started, or even worse.

Let me say this just as plainly as I can: nothing is less

intimidating to Satan than human willpower. He's defeated it a gazillion times without even working up a sweat. He squashes macho men (and women) the same way we step on ants. Even the apostle Paul, a tough dude if there ever was one, knew this to be true. He said, "I don't really understand myself, for I want to do what is right, but I don't do it. Instead, I do what I hate" (Romans 7:15). Trust me. The more confident we are in our own strength, the more Satan laughs at us . . . and the more fun he has humiliating us.

But there *is* someone who *does* intimidate Satan.

Someone he has never beaten.

Someone who crushes Satan like Satan crushes us.

Someone who is ready to help you change.

I'm speaking of the Holy Spirit, the Counselor (*NIV*) and Advocate (*NLT*) whom Jesus promised to send (John 14:16). If you let him have complete control of your life, he will transform you into the person you want to be. Paul, the same guy who admitted he didn't have the willpower to be what he wanted to be, said this: "The Holy Spirit produces this kind of fruit in our lives: love, joy, peace, patience, kindness, goodness, faithfulness, gentleness, and self-control" (Galatians 5:22, 23).

Don't skim over the first part of that verse too quickly!

If you know your sugar-and-spice reputation has been running short on sugar, you might knuckle down and start trying to be more patient, kind, gentle, and so on. But look again at what Paul said: "The Holy Spirit produces this kind of fruit in our lives." It is *not* your job to work harder and try to produce these qualities in your daily life, even though you may feel that it is. It is the Holy Spirit's job. *Your* job is to relinquish control of your life to the Holy Spirit so he can do his work.

If you set out to be more patient and gentle and kind, you'll probably succeed until the Queen of Rude crosses your path and lives up to her reputation. Then you'll blow. But if you forget about trying to be more patient and gentle and kind and just focus on surrendering to the Lord and getting as close to him as you possibly can through prayer, Bible study, worship, and service, you're going to wake up someday and discover that you're not the same person. When a self-proclaimed diva crosses your path and does something blatantly obnoxious, you'll have a completely different reaction without even trying.

Yes, that's right. Without even trying! Because it won't be you producing the fruit of patience and kindness; it will be the Holy Spirit. This is why when you surrender more and more to the Holy Spirit, you often shock yourself and your friends and family. Situations arise that would normally produce a meltdown, and it doesn't happen. The key is allowing the Holy Spirit to have and maintain control.

Recently, I bought a new car. One of the big selling points for me was a new safety feature called Electronic Stability Control, a computerized technology that helps stabilize and straighten out the car when it goes into a skid. As many as ten thousand fatal accidents a year could be prevented if every car in America were equipped with it.[32] Marilyn and I decided it was worth the extra cost.

But something interesting happened when I picked up the car. As the salesman was acquainting me with the car's bells and whistles, he said, "And this button here will disengage the Electronic Stability Control."

Puzzled, I asked, "Why would I want to do that?"

He answered, "Because sometimes you might want to have complete control of the car all by yourself and not have the computer holding you back."

And this is the problem you'll run into with the Holy Spirit. Sometimes you'll want to disengage him so he doesn't "hold you back." But the Holy Spirit doesn't come with an on/off button you can hit every time your mood changes. True surrender is ongoing, not intermittent.

Let me encourage you to seek change not through willpower but through surrender. Repent of your sin, give the Holy Spirit control of your life, and let him do his thing. You and everyone in your world will be happier.

A Time to Repair

The final step is to go back and repair, if possible, the key relationships you have damaged. I say "key relationships" because if you've been catty for a long time, there's no way you'll ever be able to track down everyone you've hurt or offended. I know women who have terrorized receptionists, sales clerks, and waitresses from coast to coast for decades. If that's you, then you just have to repent and give it all to God. But if you have family members, neighbors, friends, or coworkers whom you know have suffered because of your nasty disposition, you need to do what you can to make things right.

Let me offer four helpful repair tactics you can use. These tactics work well whether the relationships you need to repair are with men or with women, but here I'm specifically addressing relationships with other women that have been damaged by a catty spirit.

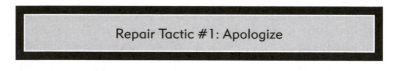

Repair Tactic #1: Apologize

Start off with an apology. It would be best to do this in person, but if circumstances don't allow a face-to-face meeting, write a letter. Whatever you do, don't make excuses for your bad behavior. Simply confess your sin and ask for forgiveness. I can tell you that an apology humbly offered can be very powerful. I remember weeping one time when someone who had made my life miserable for years asked me to forgive him. It was a day I never thought I'd see . . . and a day I'll never forget.

Apologizing is hard. But this is where you stand to gain a degree of peace and reclaim your self-respect. You could also save someone else's soul. Does that sound dramatic? Think about it: if the person you mistreated has been hating you ever since, your apology could be the catalyst for that individual to finally let go of her grudge, removing the obstacle blocking her way to God.

Yes, you need to apologize if at all possible. You can't go back and undo the damage your razor-sharp tongue and hot temper may have caused, but by doing the hard thing, you give God something he can work with.

Repair Tactic #2: Ask for and Expect Nothing in Return

The person you're apologizing to will likely be suspicious. If you've been mean to her forever and all of a sudden you show up wanting to embark on a whole new kind of relationship, she'll think you've got ulterior motives.

Let's face it, it's easy to apologize when we want or need something. That's why you mustn't say anything that might make your apology seem disingenuous or, worse yet, part of a manipulative master plan. The only thing worse than no apology at all would be one that is insincere.

Repair Tactic #3: Be Prepared to Be Tested

Don't be surprised if the woman you're apologizing to intentionally hits one of your hot buttons just to see how you react. It's only natural for someone you've terrorized to want to see if the new you is for real. The very worst thing you could do would be to allow yourself to be sucked into an old argument. I recommend that you not even think about apologizing to anyone in person until you are 100 percent sure you can take any shot across your bow without firing back.

Repair Tactic #4: When You've Done What You Can, Let It Go

If the person doesn't accept your apology or still seems angry or suspicious, that's not your problem. If you've done your best to set things right, you can walk away with a clear conscience and let God handle the rest. Romans 12:18 says, "Do all that you can to live in peace with everyone." That's all God will ever ask of you.

I had this chapter about half written when I stumbled across a book that had me staring in disbelief. At first I thought I must be hallucinating, or perhaps I had stepped through a portal in the cosmos and tumbled into a parallel universe where all truth was turned completely upside down. I blinked, rubbed my eyes, and looked again. The book was entitled *Why Men Love Bitches*.

Of course, the very idea is absurd. I would come closer to believing that doctors have started prescribing large quantities of cheese fries for their heart patients or that Dr. James Dobson has gotten a Metallica tattoo, grown a ponytail, and started dating Madonna.

I knew there had to be a catch, so I picked up the book and opened it to the introduction. Sure enough. On the very first page I found these words: "So why do men love bitches? An important distinction should be made between the pejorative way the word is usually used, and the way it is used here. Certainly, I'm not recommending that a woman have an abrasive disposition. . . . The woman I'm describing is kind, yet strong."[33]

Somebody—the author, the publisher, *somebody*—ought to be ashamed. Essentially, the author is saying, "I know my title's assertion is absurd, but I'm using it anyway because all I care about is selling books. I reserve the right to do whatever it takes, even if it means manipulating and changing the meanings of words, in order to create buzz."

Whatever happened to saying what you mean and meaning what you say? How sad is it when you have to use the very first page of your book to explain to your readers that you tricked them . . . that the book they're holding is not at all what they thought it was when they picked it up?

Here's the unadulterated truth with no word games and no tricks: Men do *not* fall in love with women who are abrasive, disagreeable, and downright mean to other women. They run away from them.

So Much More Than Sexy

Do you ever feel jealous or envious of other women? Do you feel as if you have to compete with other women in your orbit? Do you feel that you generally get along better with men than you do with women? Thinking of the people you struggle to get along with, are they mostly men, mostly women, or an equal mixture of both?

Have you ever been told that you are a hard person to get along with? If so, what evidence could you give to counter the charge?

If you sense, deep down, that you have some "catty" in you, what do you think is the root of that spirit—your upbringing? bitterness? competitiveness? Can you name the women who have suffered the most from your disposition? What, specifically, could you do to repair those relationships?

6

Male Repellent

I am going to let you in on a little secret: It may not be him. It may be you. He may not be a jerk. And he's not necessarily afraid of commitment. He may only be afraid of a commitment with you.

— Travis Stork

The purpose of this book is not to tell you how to find, attract, or snag a man. On the other hand, I do think it's important that you know what drives men away. We've already looked at how your relationships with women can make men run the other way. In this chapter I want to focus on your behavior with men.

I can think of four ways this knowledge could come in handy.

First, if you're married but sense that the relationship is growing stale, you can use this information to check yourself and make sure you're not slipping into some bad habits.

Second, if you're still single long after you hoped you would be married, you can use this information to check yourself and make sure you're not torpedoing your dreamboats before they even have a chance to sail into your harbor.

Third, if you're young and just starting to date, you can use this information to check yourself and make sure you don't blow your first chance at love. (My wife is one of many women who ended up marrying the first man she dated.)

And fourth, if you're committed to avoiding all romantic entanglements, you can use this information to check yourself and make sure you're suitably repulsive to every male who ventures near your airspace.

Male repellent doesn't come in an aerosol can or a tube.

But make no mistake—it is something you can "wear." And if you do, you won't have to worry about men bothering you. They will avoid you like a pickpocket steers clear of the cops.

In case you're wondering, I understand that there's female repellent too. I'm fully aware that guys do things that drive women away. But this is not a book to men from a woman; it's a book to women from a man. And because I am not qualified to be a spokesperson for women, I'll just be traveling in one direction on this two-way street. I'll let one of you write the book about female repellent.

Also—and this is very important—I want you to know I believe that most of the Christian women who wear male repellent do so unwittingly. I've met and talked to many of them, and I usually come away with the feeling that they don't realize how scary they appear to males. Often they are genuinely mystified as to why they can't attract or keep a guy. That's why I consider this whole book, but especially the next two chapters, to be a kind of public service.

That's right; I said the next *two* chapters. In this chapter, I'm going to tackle three common male repellents. The fourth is so powerful, so extreme, and so deadly that I think it deserves its own chapter.

So let's get to it.

Male Repellent #1: Male Bashing

I hate chain letters. I would like to say I never read them, but that wouldn't quite be true. I have read a few . . . enough to know I hate them. At one point a few years ago, I swore I would never read another one as long as I lived. But then a friend who also hates chain letters sent me one and urged me to take a look at it. I now pass it on to you:

> This letter was started with the intention of bringing hope to discouraged and discontented women around the world. Just send a copy of this letter to five of your female friends who are as unhappy as you are.
>
> Then bundle up your husband or boyfriend and send him to the woman whose name appears at the top of the list and add your name to the bottom of the list. When your name gets to the top, you should receive 15,625 men. One of them is bound to be better than the one you have. As of this writing, a friend of mine has received 184 men, one of which is halfway decent.
>
> Remember, breaking the chain will bring you bad luck. One woman I know broke the chain and got her old husband back. Whatever you do, don't break the chain!

If you think that's funny, I'm sure you'll love this other Internet gem:

> After many years of scientific research and philosophical debate, the perfect male has finally been identified. It's Mr. Potato Head! He's tan. He's cute. He understands

the importance of accessorizing. And when he looks at another woman you can rearrange his face.

Or how about this one:

> How to impress a woman:
> Wine her, dine her, call her, hug her, hold her,
> surprise her, compliment her, smile at her,
> laugh with her, cry with her, cuddle with her,
> shop with her, give her jewelry, buy her flowers,
> hold her hand, write love letters to her,
> go to the end of the earth and back for her.
>
> How to impress a man:
> Show up naked and bring beer.

Male bashing is one of the most unsexy and ungodly things a woman can do, but also (apparently) one of the most fun. It's hard to find even a tiny corner of modern culture where men are not routinely beaten to a pulp. Even the greeting card companies show us no mercy. I somehow had the idea that greeting card companies were in the business of spreading cheer and helping people feel better. How silly of me. On a recent trip to my local discount store, I stopped by the card section and found dozens of cards that were blatantly insulting to men. A typical one said, in big letters on the front, "Warning! This card contains big words. Please ask a woman to read it to you."

Oh, and for the record, I found no cards so blatantly

insulting to women, children, blacks, Hispanics, Jews, Muslims, or any other group.

And what about sitcoms?

I rarely watch one, but almost every time I do I see the leading male portrayed as a bumbling, clueless, insensitive idiot. Recently I watched an episode of *Everybody Loves Raymond* in which Raymond felt jealous of his wife's male aerobics instructor. Naturally, this compelled him to act like a moron throughout the show. He was petulant and rude to his wife (who was, of course, perfectly sweet and normal in every way). Predictably, at the end Raymond finished off the male-as-nitwit stereotype by crashing his wife's aerobics class and trying to keep up with the ladies. As they snapped crisply through their exercise routines with the precision of a Broadway chorus line, he flailed and staggered like a drunken sailor.

Sadly, we don't even get a break from the onslaught during commercials; one after another they present an unflattering portrayal of the American male. Perhaps you'll remember the one with a young man and woman sitting on a couch, their body language telling us that they're falling in love and it's time for the first kiss. Slowly, tentatively, they lean toward each other, pursing their lips for that once-in-a-lifetime, unforgettable moment. Then we hear a *ding!* off camera, which means Southwest Airlines has just sent an update about lower fares. The young man's lips are just centimeters from his girlfriend's, but his eyes pop open and he jumps up and flies out of the room to check his e-mail, while the girl loses her balance and flops awkwardly onto the carpet.

Or how about the commercial with the young wife in the bathroom checking her pregnancy test while her hubby is in the kitchen checking the beer in the refrigerator. (Coors apparently has a label that turns blue when the beer reaches optimum drinking temperature.) Simultaneously, they shout with joy—she because she's pregnant and he because his beer is ready to drink. When she realizes his joy has everything to do with his beer and nothing to do with her, she goes running out of the room in tears and slams the door. Her husband is left standing there, wondering what the big deal is.

Seriously, if you took all the commercials with stupid, insensitive, moronic males off TV, there would be very few commercials left.

As I was doing research for this chapter, I worked my way through the blogosphere, reading what real people had to say about male bashing. What I found was disheartening. Many of the discussion groups (even those on male-oriented Web sites) are dominated by females who show no mercy. A few are sympathetic, but most are downright cold. The overriding message is: if you guys don't want to be treated like idiots, quit acting like idiots.

It hasn't always been this way. If you're old enough, you'll remember when guys were generally well thought of. The TV shows *Father Knows Best*, *The Andy Griffith Show*, *The*

Brady Bunch, and others depicted men in a positive way. But when the feminist movement got rolling in the '60s, things began to change. At the 1968 Miss America Pageant, feminist protestors threw their bras (symbols of female oppression) into the trash can.[34] A couple of years later, Archie Bunker showed up in prime time as the king of TV nincompoops, and it was all downhill from there. It's as if someone fired a starter's pistol and said, "Let the bashing begin!"

Now, I know most of my readers are not going to be hard-core male bashers. It's more than likely that you are a Christian and can see the sin in trashing any group of people. But you might be what I would call a soft-core male basher; that is, you might be the kind of woman who is quick to laugh at an anti-male joke, or to tell one. You might be the kind of woman whose body language says volumes: the rolling eyes, the shaking head, the sigh of exasperation every time a man messes up. Worst of all, you might be the kind of woman who condescends to men . . . who talks about them (and *to* them) as if they were little boys.

Men do not like this.

Let me rephrase that.

Men *hate* this. We do not want to be in the same area code with women who treat us this way.

No, I'm not saying we don't occasionally do dumb things. Sometimes our antics deserve a good roll of the eyes or a funny one-liner. But the relentless pounding, even if it's not always brutal and sadistic, gets old real quick.

I'm sure you've heard of the Proverbs 31 woman. She's been the subject of countless books and sermons because she epitomizes what a godly woman should be. In fact, I've learned that many of you feel a little uncomfortable with her because she sets the standard so high. I like her, however, and I think most men who read about her do also, partly because of what this verse says about the way she treats her man: "She brings him good, not harm, all the days of her life" (v. 12, *NIV*).

No wonder the husband of this ideal woman adored her so. Verses 28, 29 say, "Her husband praises her: 'There are many virtuous and capable women in the world, but you surpass them all!'"

Here is the plain, unvarnished truth: No guy wants to be a punching bag. It's not fun, sexy, godly, or anything else we're interested in. So bash us if you want, but know that if you do, we will run the other way.

Male Repellent #2: Drama

Men are often accused of being inattentive, of tuning out and not listening to their wives or girlfriends. And at times we're guilty. I've been known to expand my hearing to include the baseball scores coming from the TV as my wife tries to tell me what kind of cereal to pick up at the grocery store. But often we're not as guilty as we might seem. Sometimes our attention deficit is in fact a defense mechanism. When the volume of words flying at us reaches blizzard status, when the situation being discussed is not a crisis and does not justify said blizzard, and especially when we've heard it all before (a dozen times), our listening apparatus flashes "Overload" and automatically shuts down. It's not that we don't love you or care about your problems. It's that we are not into drama. Never have been and never will be. God just didn't wire us that way.

Cultural proof of man's general inability to stomach a lot of drama is indicated by the fact that you never hear anyone talking about a drama king. Drama *queens*, on the other hand, are at least plentiful enough to have spawned the cliché.

If you need a Bible verse, think about Solomon. The dude had seven hundred wives and three hundred concubines. You think maybe—just maybe—there were a few drama queens among them? If only one in ten were drama queens, that would make one hundred of them in Solomon's orbit. That could be why he said, "The more words you speak, the less they mean. So what good are they?" (Ecclesiastes 6:11).

But I want to stress that it's not the talking; it's the drama.

- It's the turning of molehills into mountains, the fretting and stewing over every little thing that happens.

- It's the crying, the yelling, and the pouting. (Oh, how we hate the pouting!)
- It's the exaggerating and the overreacting, the never-ending phone calls and text messages.
- It's the constant sense of persecution.

Worst of all, it's the insinuation that if we choose not to get caught up in the whirlwind, we are insensitive and uncaring.

The truth is, we may seem insensitive and uncaring, but we are probably just tired.

- Tired of being dragged from one perceived crisis to another.
- Tired of the gossip, the exaggerations, and the hysteria.
- Tired of the mood swings.
- Tired of walking on eggshells.
- Tired of feeling like every conversation is a debate over the death penalty.
- And yes, tired of getting our chops busted for being tired.

Most of the guys I know are *very* interested in what their women are thinking, feeling, and doing. But there comes a point at which everything that can be said has been said, everything that can be analyzed has been analyzed, and everything that can be done has been done. At that point the drama queen is just getting warmed up good. The guy, however, is ready to go bungee jumping without a bungee.

I've known quite a few drama queens in my time, and I always have the same thought: *She reminds me of junior high*. Most girls are drama queens at that age. Talk to any seventh- or eighth-grade teacher and you'll hear it. The Pentagon doesn't see as many plots and subplots in a year as a junior high school does in a week. Thankfully, the vast majority of women grow well beyond that level of maturity. The ones who don't usually bounce from boyfriend to boyfriend or, even worse, from husband to husband.

Yes, drama queens almost always end up alone. It doesn't matter how beautiful you are—if you habitually blow everything out of proportion, your man will eventually leave you or at least withdraw. Proverbs 21:9 says, "It's better to live alone in the corner of an attic than with a quarrelsome wife in a lovely home." I don't know a single man who's ever been married to a drama queen who wouldn't shout a hearty amen to that verse.

Some guys start out thinking otherwise. They convince themselves that a little drama is a small price to pay if the girl rates a ten in the looks department. But eventually even these guys start looking for a way out. Though they may choose not to break up or divorce because of the children or religious convictions, they still withdraw emotionally. You go through enough drama and the corner of that attic starts looking pretty good.

I once counseled a true drama queen. I mean, she was

to drama queens what Tiger Woods is to golfers. The queen of the queens. Her husband had basically become an emotional vegetable. She even called him comatose when she described his interaction with her. And I understood. Figuratively speaking, he had chosen to live in the corner of the attic.

I remember sitting at my desk before she arrived, wondering what I could say to her that might make some sense. I picked up my Bible and started flipping through it. I prayed, "Lord, got any ideas on how I can approach this woman?" At almost that instant, I came to Luke 10, and my eyes settled on the story of Jesus' visit to his two female friends, Mary and Martha.

You probably recall how Mary sat at Jesus' feet, listening to him and soaking up his presence, while her sister cooked dinner, fuming because she wasn't getting any help and banging the pots and pans a little louder than necessary to make sure Jesus and her lazy sister knew how ticked she was. Martha's behavior was classic drama queen: take everything personally, create a problem where none exists, and above all, make sure everybody knows how hurt you feel.

If you have a version of the Bible with Jesus' words in red, you'll notice that the entire story is in black except for the words Jesus spoke to Martha. Maybe that's why they caught my eye. Or maybe the Lord was just answering my prayer. At any rate, here's what Jesus said: "My dear

Martha, you are worried and upset over all these details! There is only one thing worth being concerned about. Mary has discovered it, and it will not be taken away from her" (vv. 41, 42).

If you even suspect you might have a drama queen bent, you need to pray over those words. Substitute your name for Martha's and ask God to help you discern the things in your life that are not worth getting upset over. And when you identify them, let them go. You'll be happier, you'll be godlier, and you'll certainly be more attractive.

Male Repellent #3: Nagging

If you look up the word *nag* in the dictionary, you'll see that it's listed as both a verb and a noun. The verb means to badger, berate, or pester. The noun refers to a person who nags. Some dictionaries even specify that the person is usually female! Experience tells me this is true. In the years I have been in the ministry, I have never heard one wife accuse her husband of being a nag. Not one. But I have heard hundreds of husbands complain about their nagging wives.

Of course, the wives almost always plead innocent. They claim that they're not *nagging* their husbands; they're *helping* them. They recognize flaws in their men that need to be corrected, and they think that if they harp on them long enough, they'll eventually see some changes. Most women say that they hate nagging. What they mean is that they hate *having* to nag. They would like to see their men straighten up of their own accord. But I know some women who appear to love nagging. Even when their husbands are ship-shape and doing nothing wrong, they can find something to pick at.

By the way, most people don't know that nagging was once a crime. Up until the nineteenth century, there were laws in both the United States and Europe that allowed husbands to press charges against their wives for nagging. If the woman was found guilty, she faced the same punishment witches and prostitutes had to endure—being strapped to a seat, dunked in a river or a lake, and held underwater for a predetermined length of time. The number of dunkings depended on the severity of the offense or the number of previous offenses.[35]

For the record, I'm glad those laws are no longer on the books. But be advised: you will still suffer if you nag. I can think of three bad things that will probably happen.

Bad Thing #1: Your Man Will Dig in His Heels

In fact, many guys feel this is the only real option they have. They figure that if they buckle under to the nagging, their women will think, *Wow! This really works!* and will do it even more.

But don't expect your man to be blatantly defiant. Rather than telling you off, he'll probably just start erecting walls. He'll find other things to do, he'll take longer to do those things, he'll work late, he'll be tired, he won't feel well . . . anything to keep you from winning.

Bad Thing #2: Your Man Will Have Second Thoughts About Your Relationship

Think about it. If someone constantly picks at you, you're eventually going to assume she doesn't like you for who you are. And very quickly on the heels of that thought, you're going to wonder if you even want to be in a relationship with a woman who doesn't like you for who you are.

At this point, I need to say something about the make-over mentality a lot of women seem to have. That's when you think, *A man is like a house. I don't see him for what he is; I see him for what he will be when I finish remodeling him.*

If you think that way, you're almost certain to nag your man and just as likely to drive him away. No guy wants to be thought of as a fixer-upper. We know we have stuff we need to work on, that we can always grow and get better. But it's insulting and wounding to be constantly told that we're inadequate.

Bad Thing #3: Your Man Will Notice Other Women Who Are Not Nags

I'm convinced this is how a lot of affairs start. It's not so much that guys are looking for a different sex partner. It's that when they're constantly nagged at home, they are inevitably drawn to anybody who seems to like them for who they are. Often, sex is the furthest thing from their minds. They just enjoy being in the company of someone who doesn't talk down to them and who isn't constantly trying to fix them. Then as the friendship develops, temptations start to arise.

You might be thinking I'm blaming wives for their husbands' infidelity. That's not it at all. There is no excuse for unfaithfulness, none whatsoever. But it's foolish and naive to think that certain behaviors don't drive wedges into relationships and create opportunities for Satan to slip in and do his work.

If you're a nagger, stop before you drive your man so far away that you can never get him back. Change your focus. Instead of zeroing in on his frailties and imperfections, think about why you were attracted to this man in the first place. The apostle Paul said, "Fix your thoughts on what is true, and honorable, and right, and pure, and lovely, and admirable. Think about things that are excellent and worthy of praise" (Philippians 4:8).

Aren't there things about your man that are honorable and admirable? If so, lock in on them and enjoy them. Hopefully, the two of you can grow together and both become better people over time.

～～～～～

I read somewhere that mice and humans share 95 percent of the same DNA. (So I guess that old question "Are you a man or a mouse?" isn't as far-fetched as it first seems.) Compare a human and a mouse in your mind. Wouldn't you swear that we are only 5 percent the same rather than 5 percent different?

As I was laying out this chapter, I found myself wondering what the difference is, not between a human and a mouse, but between a woman men are attracted to and a woman men run from. I believe the difference is very, very small. Often, one attitude or habit is all it takes to scare a man away. That attitude or habit may not even be visible at times. It could be the kind of thing that only rears its head occasionally. But that's the thing about repellents: they're powerful. You don't have to dip yourself in a vat of mosquito repellent to send the tiny dive-bombers searching for another target. A few squirts do the trick.

This might sound like bad news, but it's actually good news. If there's very little difference between women men are attracted to and women they're not attracted to, that means you could move from the latter category to the former fairly easily and quickly. If you understand the power of repellents and are honest enough to admit that you're wearing one, it could actually be a pretty quick fix.

Bottom line: If guys seem to be steering clear of you (or grabbing parachutes and flinging themselves out the hatch shortly after takeoff), you don't need a shrink or a miracle bra or cosmetic surgery. You probably need to wash off that repellent.

The three in this chapter, and one more. . . .

So Much More Than Sexy

When you hear a male-bashing comment or joke, do you find yourself keeping quiet or jumping in quickly to laugh and agree? Do you commonly make statements that lump all guys into one category?

Do you find that drama is relatively rare or relatively common in your life? Do most of your conversations have to do with what's going on in *your* life? Has your husband or boyfriend ever accused you of being a nag? Were you offended? Did you argue? If so, what makes you think you're *not* a nag?

In general, do you sense men being drawn to you or moving away from you? What do you think that says about the "smell" of your attitude? What needs to change to make you less repellent and more godly?

7

The Radioactive Woman

If you're bolting through your single life just trying . . .
to find some way out of it before you turn thirty, or thirty-five,
or forty, or whatever age you've arbitrarily chosen,
you are going to wind up married to a crocodile head.

—Linda Holmes

Men can be pretty slow to pick up on things. Sometimes you have to draw us a picture. But the one thing we are never slow to pick up on is desperation, or as I like to call it: emotional radiation, the ultimate male repellent.

When a desperate female enters a man's airspace, his internal Geiger counter starts clicking like mad. Nerve and brain impulses start firing. All of his internal machinery suddenly shifts into reverse. He'll start backing up, looking for the closest exit, faking food poisoning . . . anything to get away. The only person who's drawn to a desperate woman is an equally desperate man. But if you're single, I assume that's not the kind of guy you're looking for. I assume you *don't* want to go through life with the universal symbol for radioactivity tattooed on your forehead. I assume that you don't want to go through life seeing every nice man you meet go running away from you. That's why I decided to devote a chapter to this subject. That and my conviction that a desperate woman is the polar opposite of the woman who's pursing godly.

An entire segment of the publishing industry seems devoted to cultivating this quality of desperation in single women. On a recent sojourn to my local megabookstore, I found dozens of "radioactive" titles in the relationship section, including these:

- *Secrets of the Ultimate Husband Hunter*
- *Will He Really Leave Her for Me?*
- *Make Every Man Want You*

- *How to Attract Anyone, Anytime, Anyplace*
- *Flirt Speak: The Sexy Language of Flirting*
- *Read My Hips: The Sexy Art of Flirtation*
- *101 Ways to Flirt*
- *How to Flirt*
- *Flirting 101*
- *Superflirt*
- *The Flirt Coach*
- *The Flirt Coach's Secrets of Attraction*
- *The Flirt Coach's Guide to Finding the Love You Want*

And my personal choice for radioactive book of the year: *1001 Ways to Meet Mr. Right* by Elizabeth Shimer Bowers, which serves up 1001 suggestions on where a girl can hang out in hopes of finding the man of her dreams. As I flipped through the book, I didn't know whether to laugh or cry. Some of the more interesting (read that: pathetic) suggestions are these (with my own comments in parentheses):

#22: a tattoo parlor (Doesn't every girl want a guy who appreciates the arts?)

#26: a bar near a hospital (to try to snag a rich doctor unwinding at the end of a long, hard day)

#119: a maternity ward (because new parents have brothers who will stop by to see their new nieces and nephews)

#185: a Hooters restaurant (because everybody knows guys love wings)

#246: a condom store (because any guy who doesn't settle for plain old drugstore Trojans obviously appreciates the finer things in life)

#248: the tool section of a department store (What says romance more than some hacksaw blades and a few drill bits?)

#246: a strip club (because really, who wouldn't love to have a boyfriend who's into strippers?)

#255: a used car lot (because men love cars and there are both shoppers *and* salesmen you can hit on)

#425: YouTube (because if you date a guy who advertised himself to the opposite sex with a homemade movie, you are guaranteed not to be the most desperate person in the relationship)

#989: a nude beach (At least you won't have to worry about what to wear.)

You might be wondering why the publishing industry seems so bent on spreading emotional radioactivity throughout the female population. Simple. They know that desperate females will get themselves caught up in disastrous relationships, which will naturally create a whole new market for a different kind of book. Hence, the following titles were sitting right alongside the aforementioned ones at the same bookstore:

- *Dump That Chump*
- *I Used to Miss Him . . . but My Aim Is Improving*
- *Hit Him Where It Hurts*
- *Lose That Loser and Find the Right Guy*
- *He Had It Coming*
- *When Your Lover Is a Liar*
- *How Could You Do This to Me?*
- *Dating Sucks: What to Do When Your Love Life Makes You Miserable*
- *Let's Face It, Men Are @$$#%\¢$*

Do you see how this works? Desperate woman goes to bookstore. Desperate woman buys book. Desperate woman gains new confidence and formulates new strategy. Desperate woman employs strategy and gets pathetic male to date her. Relationship crashes and burns. Desperate woman is emotionally distraught. Desperate woman goes back to bookstore. Desperate woman buys a different kind of book.

I'm telling you, it's all a conspiracy perpetrated in the boardrooms of America's great publishing houses. Just as surely as God made little green apples, desperation sells books—both on the front end and the back end—and those wily publishers know it. Of course, they would tell you that they're just meeting a need, but don't kid yourself. The more radioactive you are, the better they like it. So I have to ask, wouldn't it be better if you could just stop being desperate?

- Think how much happier you would be.
- Think about all the plotting and scheming you wouldn't have to do.
- Think about all the pathetic men you wouldn't have to pretend to like.
- Think about all the self-loathing you wouldn't feel.
- Think about all the decent men who wouldn't treat you like you had the Ebola virus.
- Think how much less you would spend on books.

Honestly, I've never known a desperate *and* happy woman. Not even one. So if you know you have this problem, keep reading. I'm going to spend the balance of this chapter showing you how to unlock the prison door and set yourself free.

Are You Radioactive?

Just because you're single and want to be in a relationship doesn't mean you're desperate. (You were wired that way by God.) Just because you've dated a few losers doesn't mean you're desperate. (Who hasn't?) And just because you've perused the relationship section of your local bookstore doesn't mean you're desperate. (There are good books there too.) There are, however, some surefire indicators that no single male is safe within one hundred yards of you. Have a mirror handy as you read through the list and see what your heart tells you.

Indicator #1: You Try Too Hard

I won't belabor this because I hammered it hard in chapter 1, but if you're truly desperate you try too hard with your looks. You obsess over every little physical flaw because one might be the deal breaker for Prince Charming. So if there's a way to color it, camouflage it, lift it, stretch it, flatten it, tighten it, or pump it up, you'll find it.

The one thing you will *not* do is ignore it. You believe the adage about never having a second chance to make a first impression, so you never step out the door of your house, even to pick up the paper from the driveway, unless every aspect of your appearance is shipshape. After all, your long-lost soul mate could be walking his dog past your house at that very moment!

But you also try too hard to get a relationship going.

You offer the guy your phone number before he asks for it. You give him your e-mail address. You drop hints the size of the Hindenburg to let him know you're available 24/7 if he should ever want to go out with you. You laugh hysterically at every little joke he makes (even if it's not funny), and you tell him how you've always been attracted to guys with a sense of humor. You compliment him on everything he wears, no matter how bad you think he looks. Worst of all, you joke about your "ticking clock" and tell him that you've already picked out names for your future children.

Indicator #2: You Worry Too Much

You worry about missing his call (even though he's never called you), so you keep your cell phone with you at all times, sleeping with it and turning up the ringer so you can hear it when you're in the shower. You worry about being available if he decides to ask you out, so you never make other plans. You worry about keeping your look current, so you go shopping for new clothes.

And if you're totally and pathetically desperate, you worry about whether he's seeing another girl, so you stake out his house or apartment or tail him when he leaves work.

Indicator #3: You Overlook Too Much

If he acts like a jerk, you tell yourself he's just having a bad day. If he fails to keep his word, you tell yourself he couldn't help it. If he loses his temper, you tell yourself he's under a lot of pressure. If he flirts with other girls, you tell yourself he's just kidding around. If he asks to borrow money, that's because times are tough for everybody. And if he presses you to have sex with him, that's because he loves you, of course. And if you ever get the feeling that he might not be the right guy for you, you tell yourself he's not as bad as some other guys you've dated.

Indicator #4: You Sacrifice Too Much

Your girlfriends are having a girls' night out. They're going to a movie and to eat at your favorite restaurant. They're begging you to go, but you decline because he might call and want to do something.

You're offered a nice promotion, but you turn it down because it will mean moving to another part of the building where you won't get to see him every day.

He asks if you want to eat at a restaurant you don't care for, and you say yes because you don't want him to think you're disagreeable.

He shows up at your house with a porn DVD and some naughty ideas, and you go along with them because you don't want him to think you're a prude.

He wants you to skip church so you can go to the races with him (even though he knows you hate racing). So you go, even though you know he would never consider skipping the races so he could go to church with you (even though he knows you love going to church).

Indicator #5: You Enjoy Too Little

You know in your heart that romantic relationships should be fun and fulfilling. They should not be a source of guilt and worry and frustration. Yet that seems to be mostly what you get. You see other couples who are happy and you feel sad, not because of what they have but because of what you don't have. You watch *Beauty and the Beast* and cry like a baby because even though you're in a relationship with a guy, you know you'll never experience true romance with him. And even though you understand this, you stay in the relationship because you're terrified of being alone.

Indicator #6: You Act Too Weird

The first five indicators can make an explosive concoction. Perhaps you remember astronaut Lisa Nowak, who at age forty-three flew on the space shuttle *Discovery* and operated its robotic arm during three spacewalks.[36] She was so desperate to hang onto a relationship with Navy Commander William Oefelein that she donned a trench coat and wig and drove nine hundred miles (from Houston to Orlando) to confront her perceived rival,

Colleen Shipman. Nowak found Shipman at the Orlando airport, where she followed her to her car and harassed her, banging on the car window and screaming. When Shipman lowered the window slightly, Nowak sprayed a chemical inside, causing Shipman to drive away in a panic and call the police. When Nowak was arrested, she was found to be carrying a rope, a knife, a steel mallet, and several large trash bags. She was charged with attempted kidnapping and attempted murder.

What makes this story even more tragic is that Lisa Nowak was married and the mother of three children (even married women can be radioactive). It would take a team of psychologists to figure out how such an intelligent woman with so much going for her ended up in such a dark place. But the one thing all men recognized the instant that story broke was that she was one desperate female. All of the factors that make desperation such an ugly force apparently dovetailed in her mind and pushed her over the edge.

I'm not saying you'll end up with a mug shot and a rap sheet just because you're desperate to catch and keep a man, but I *am* saying that desperation can lead you to a dark place where you become someone other than the person God intends for you to be—and someone other than the person you *want* to be. That's why you might need to do some serious soul searching right now. If you are radioactive, you've got to admit it and determine in your heart that you're going to change.

Reducing Your Radiation Level

So what can you do to reduce your desperation level and reclaim your spiritual and emotional integrity? I've got several ideas. Let's call them radiation reducers.

Radiation Reducer #1: Reflect on the Fate of Other Desperate Women You Have Known

You won't be able to think of a single desperate woman who's truly happy. Most of them will be stuck with losers. Quite a few will have gotten pregnant before marriage. Some no doubt have children by two or three guys. They probably struggle financially. If they go to church at all, they probably go alone. And their self-esteem is in the pits; they hate themselves for not making better decisions.

For many years I have watched women—many of them well-meaning Christians—throw themselves at any guy who would give them a second look. They would never admit it, but they do this because they've decided that anybody will do. They've concluded that it's better to settle than to be alone. But settling is the quickest, most direct route to misery, and there are millions of women walking around zombie-like who are living proof. Look at them closely and ask yourself, *Do I want to end up like that?*

Radiation Reducer #2: Rethink Your Need for a Man

It's only natural for you to want to be in a relationship. There's nothing wrong with keeping your eyes open and interacting in healthy ways with members of the opposite sex. But the real question is, do you absolutely need a man in your life to be happy? And if you do, what does that say about you?

I have a friend who was single until she was in her forties. She wanted to be married and have children, but she was determined not to settle. One time she told me that she didn't need a man beside her to enjoy a walk on the beach, she didn't need to be huddled next to a man to enjoy a scary movie, she didn't need to have a man sitting across from her to enjoy her favorite restaurant, and she certainly didn't need a man beside her to enjoy a good night's sleep.

She believed there were blessings available to her every day. She could either reach out and grab them or let them fly on by because of some twisted notion that blessings are only for couples. She told me she intended to have a good time with or without a man. And she did.

Maybe it's time for you to rethink some of your assumptions.

Radiation Reducer #3: Learn to Appreciate the Power of the Process

Desperate people are always in a hurry. They're in a hurry to find someone, in a hurry to get serious, in a hurry to get married, in a hurry to have kids. In my experience, this is especially true of women. There's something to that old adage about the biological clock constantly ticking in the background. As a result, there is a tendency to rush everything about the relationship. You end up kissing on the first date, having sex on the third, and deciding to move in together on the fifth. The loser boyfriend is OK with this because it means he's going to be getting sex without having to work for it. The problem is, he doesn't share your romantic illusions. He's not seeing the little house with the white picket fence and hearing the pitter-patter of little feet in his dreams. He's just wants to know what you're making for dinner and when you two can have sex again.

You need to understand that all healthy relationships develop through a natural, unrushed process. It's like building a house. Every stage of the construction has to pass an inspection before you move on to the next. If there's a flaw, you fix it. Under no circumstances do you ever just say, "Oh well, it's not a big deal" and jump to the next level. You recognize that someday the building (the relationship) is going to be battered by storms, and you know that whether it stands or collapses is going to depend on how well it was built.

Yes, I know you can point to some happy couples who had whirlwind romances. Trust me. They do not prove that what I'm saying isn't true. They simply prove that occasionally people can do it all wrong and still come out with a good result. We've all known lousy parents whose kids somehow turned out good, but that doesn't mean you should raise your kids the way they raised theirs.

Radiation Reducer #4: Be Conscious of the Signals You Send

Have you stopped to think about what your desperation really says? Doesn't it basically tell the world that you are unhappy with your life? Think about it. Why would you be so anxious to get another life if you were happy with the one you already have? And let's follow this logic a little further. If a man sees your desperation and concludes that you are leading an unhappy life, why on earth would he want to jump into it with you? That would be like a restaurant owner putting a sign in the window that says, "The Food Is Awful Here and the Service Stinks, but Please Come In and Eat." Most people would drive right on by. And most guys are going to pass right on by a woman who is obviously unhappy with her life.

One of the best things you can do for yourself is learn to be happy with the life you have. If it's not exactly what you want, work to improve it. But in the meantime, be thankful for the good things God has given you. Find joy in what you have instead of stewing over what you don't have. You'll be happier and a lot more attractive.

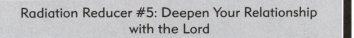

Radiation Reducer #5: Deepen Your Relationship with the Lord

Remember my single friend in her forties who, although she wanted to be married, said she didn't need a man beside her to enjoy the sweet moments of life? She also told me something else—that after many years of single living and with her soul mate nowhere in sight, she decided to let Jesus be her husband. I asked her what she meant by that because it sounded a little weird to me. She said, "I just decided to let Jesus meet the deepest needs of my heart."

When she said that, I thought of a little chorus I used to sing:

> He is all I need
> He is all I need
> Jesus is all I need . . .

That's an easy chorus to sing but not so easy to live. Yet my friend had decided to make it the theme of her life. She decided not to chase sexy but to pursue godly, and she devoted herself to Christ more wholeheartedly than ever. She surrendered her frustrations about being single. She quit worrying about trying to find her long-lost soul mate. She quit analyzing all of her physical flaws and spending money on clothes she didn't need. She kissed all of that pressure good-bye and decided just to enjoy her life in Christ—and she found a level of relief and happiness that had escaped her before.

I realize you might read this and feel sorry for her. *That poor thing. She just gave up.* No, she didn't.

You'll understand this if you think about the Levites of ancient Israel. They were appointed by God to care for the ark of the covenant and perform all ministerial duties, important work to be sure. But when it came time to divvy up the land of Canaan, the Levites didn't receive an inheritance. Instead, the Lord said to them, "I will be your inheritance" (see Numbers 18:20; Deuteronomy 10:9), and with those words he made the Levites richer than all the other tribes put together.

Pay attention to this next statement.

If the Lord is all you have, you have more than enough.

When my friend decided to let Jesus be her husband, she was acknowledging this truth. She was abandoning her desperation and saying, "Lord, if I can't find happiness with you, I'll never find it with an imperfect man." And she *did* find the happiness that had eluded her for so long. She also found a husband. I don't know . . . maybe it was because she finally quit obsessing over her singleness and reduced her radiation level. Maybe it was because God was so pleased with her devotion to him that he just decided to bless her socks off. All I know is that she looked up one day and saw her dreamboat chugging into the harbor of her heart.

I can't promise that if you do what she did, you'll find your dreamboat. But I do know this: if the Lord is all you have, you have more than enough.

You might be feeling pretty low right now. If you know in your heart that you've been radioactive, this chapter might have pulverized your self-esteem. In that case, I have two things to say to you.

First, remember that Jesus said, "You will know the truth, and the truth will set you free" (John 8:32). As painful as this chapter might have been for you to read, you needed to hear the truth. I know the truth hurts, but you were never going to be anything but miserable as long as your radiation levels were off the charts. Now you know what you need to do to plot a happier course for your life and to greatly increase the chance of a nice guy actually wanting to talk to you instead of running away.

Second, take comfort in the fact that Jesus has a soft spot

in his heart for desperate women. Remember, he knows a little something about rejection. He knows how awful it feels when someone you want to have a relationship with turns and walks away. I think that explains the tenderness he showed toward two women in particular.

One was the Samaritan woman he met at Jacob's well (John 4:5-30). Her desperation is indicated by the fact that she had been married five times and was now living with a man she wasn't married to. We don't know the details of her backstory, but that sure sounds like the résumé of a desperate woman to me. Even today, if you heard about someone who had been married and divorced five times and had a live-in boyfriend, you'd raise your eyebrows and say, "Yikes!"

Another desperate woman Jesus encountered was a woman caught in adultery (John 8:1-11). Again, we don't know how she ended up in the man's bed, but we do know she didn't belong there. We have to assume she knew the law, knew that she could be stoned to death if she was caught. Only desperation would compel her to do something she knew could get her the death penalty.

Jesus wasn't harsh with either of these women. He could have been. He could have cut loose with a dandy sermon, one that we would still be studying to this day. Instead, he showed nothing but grace and understanding.

I think he understood their pain.

And I believe he understands yours too.

Which is why you shouldn't beat yourself up. Jesus sure wouldn't. He would give you a big hug, assure you of his love, and tell you to go and be radioactive no more.

So Much More Than Sexy

What factors create a feeling of desperation in women? Have you ever sought advice on how to attract a man? Did the advice you received work? Have you ever lowered your standards just so you wouldn't have to be alone?

If you are single, what are some of the advantages? If you are married, are there some things you miss about being single? In your opinion, would it be better to be single forever or to lower your standards slightly and marry someone who isn't quite what you had in mind?

Psalm 23:1 says, "The LORD is my shepherd; I have all that I need." If you are single and wish you were married, do you bear any bitterness toward God for not bringing someone into your life? Is it hard for you to say what David said, that you have everything you need in the Lord? What are some steps you could take to allow God to fill more of the emptiness in your life?

8

Shift Happens

The great thing about being sixty is that you no longer have to close your drapes, because nobody's going to look anyway.

—Joan Rivers

I am a collector of odd books. Oddly, one of my favorite odd books is about odds, titled *Life: The Odds*.[37] While perusing this fun little treatise about research and mathematics, I ran across the following information that might interest you. The comments in parentheses are mine.

The odds that the man you're dating is a millionaire are 215 to 1. (The odds that he wants you to *think* he's a millionaire are much better.)

The odds that you will achieve sainthood in the Catholic church are 20 million to 1. (The miracle is the hard part. Once you accomplish that, you're on the fast track.)

The odds that you will win an Academy Award are 11,500 to 1. (That's *if* you manage to land a part in a movie. But don't give up hope. If Keanu Reeves can do it, we've all got a shot.)

The odds that you will die in a restaurant because nobody in the place knows the Heimlich maneuver are 5,558 to 1. (You can beat the odds by ordering soup.)

The odds of your getting hemorrhoids are 3 to 2. (Maybe you'd better keep that old pillow around after all.)

The odds of your getting away with murder are 2 to 1. (Talk to O. J. Simpson for ideas on how to improve these odds.)

The odds that you'll be audited by the IRS at some point during your lifetime are 3 to 1. (Did you save your receipt for this book?)

The odds of your striking it rich on *Antiques Roadshow* are 10,000 to 1. (But the real question is, did the person who actually struck it rich buy the item at *your* garage sale?)

And finally, what everyone wants to know: the annual odds of being struck by lightning are 576,000 to 1. (But women can breathe a little easier because 84 percent of people struck by lightning are male, probably due to the fact that many of us guys really don't have enough sense to come in out of the rain.)

Allow me to offer one more set of odds that I didn't find in that book but that seems important as I close out this book. The odds of your losing your youthful look as you grow into middle age and beyond are 1 to 1. You can slather fistfuls of industrial strength Oil of Olay on your face every day, but you will not stop the Crow's Feet Express. You can pump dumbbells and do tummy crunches religiously, but your cargo will still ride a little lower as the years go by. Like it or not, gravity always wins. Shift happens.

The question is, how are you going to handle it? Or how *are* you handling it?

You've got lots of options, you know. Lots of *bad* options that will not help you in your pursuit of godly.

For example, you could take the Joan Rivers approach and have your skin stretched so tightly over your face that your eyebrows end up in different voting precincts. You could take the Barbara Walters approach and write a tell-all book revealing the sexual escapades of your youth to make people think you're more fun than you really are. Or you could take the Demi Moore approach and find yourself a boyfriend young enough to be your son. Shift will still happen no matter which of these approaches you take, but you might be able to create enough of a diversion that no one will notice right away.

Even if you do stave off (temporarily) the image and appearance issues that aging creates, you still have to deal with the aches and pains. This was illustrated recently when Tina Turner and Cher appeared on *The Oprah Winfrey Show*. Tina was sixty-eight and Cher was sixty-one at the time, but there they sat, looking all youthful and glamorous. And I *do* mean youthful. If you put all their wrinkles end to end, they wouldn't total two inches. Their hair was wild and sexy (Cher's was blonde), and Tina even chose a daring neckline (for someone her age) that bared one shoulder. Everyone marveled at their youthful looks, which seemed to be the point of the show. However, the telltale moment came when Oprah asked Tina and Cher how they felt about aging. Cher piped up and said, "I think it sucks!" What? Could it be that the wrinkleless wonder has developed a cantankerous colon? Or that the infamous arthritis gremlin has set up shop in her left knee and is doing a booming business?

Surprise, surprise.

You might as well face the fact that you cannot stop what time has planned for your body. You might find ways to delay the inevitable for a little while, but even then you must be very careful that you don't end up looking ridiculous. Who hasn't seen the pathetic creature at the mall or the grocery store who turns heads for all the wrong reasons? You know the woman I'm talking about—the sixty-year-old grandma who apparently believes her baggy knees, liver spots, flabby belly, dry skin, and sagging breasts suddenly become invisible when she puts on short shorts and a tank top. Reminds me of the joke about the old woman who put on a peekaboo top. Men peeked . . . and then booed.

No, you cannot stop what time has planned for your body, but (with apologies to Dylan Thomas) neither do you have to go soft into that good night. Women who decide to pursue godly can carry their so-much-more-than-sexy lifestyle right on through middle age and into their golden years because they understand where the key battle has to be fought and won. It's not at the dinner table, the fitness center, or the hair salon. It's between your ears.

The apostle Paul wrote, "Don't copy the behavior and customs of this world, but let God transform you into a new person by changing the way you think" (Romans 12:2). One behavior and custom of this world is to fight the aging process with sit-ups, hair color, miraculous undergarments, the latest fad diet, Botox, or surgery. Women spend untold sums of money every year, desperately trying to hang on to the body they used to have. Paul said that the key to becoming a new and better person is getting the right thoughts churning in your brain.

Even some in the secular world are starting to figure this out. Look at these words from Suzanne Somers: "These are the people whose lives have gone off track because they are foolishly chasing their youth instead of accepting change. But life is a flow and we must follow it wherever it leads us. The happiest people are those who can put this into a positive perspective. Everything you think you have lost is really your opportunity to gain. It's looking at the glass as half full instead of half empty."[38]

She's absolutely right. The critical battleground is the mind. The only thing I would add is that the "positive perspective" she speaks of needs to come from God. Remember Paul's words? "Let God transform you into a new person by changing the way you think." Emphasis on God.

How does God change our thinking? Through his Word. Second Timothy 3:16 says, "All Scripture is inspired by God and is useful to teach us what is true and to make us realize what is wrong in our lives. It corrects us when we are wrong and teaches us to do what is right."

Did you catch that?

It corrects us when we are wrong.

If your thoughts about aging are tangled . . . if the realization that your time is rapidly shrinking while your hips are rapidly expanding has thrown you into a cold sweat, allow me to point you toward a simple Bible truth that will straighten out your thinking and give you some peace.

Solomon's Secret #1

The Book of Ecclesiastes is weird. Some might even say it's schizophrenic. For example, it was written by a really smart guy (King Solomon), but it chronicles his really dumb mistakes. It's both sarcastic and serious. It speaks of regret but urges resolve. It oozes despair but offers hope. It's the only book in the Bible that sounds like lyrics to a country song one minute and a high-powered motivational speech the next. Solomon must have been in some kind of mood when he wrote it.

But schizophrenic or not, it's an important book, especially for women who've been sucker punched by Father Time and are trying to regain their balance. Solomon's secret of aging well is tucked neatly into this passage about time, Ecclesiastes 3:1-8, easily the most famous in the book:

> For everything there is a season,
> a time for every activity under heaven.
> A time to be born and a time to die.
> A time to plant and a time to harvest.
> A time to kill and a time to heal.
> A time to tear down and a time to build up.
> A time to cry and a time to laugh.
> A time to grieve and a time to dance.
> A time to scatter stones and a time to gather stones.
> A time to embrace and a time to turn away.
> A time to search and a time to quit searching.
> A time to keep and a time to throw away.

A time to tear and a time to mend.
A time to be quiet and a time to speak.
A time to love and a time to hate.
A time for war and a time for peace.

Solomon was no spring chicken when he wrote those words. He was looking back over a long, active life and making some poignant observations. No doubt a range of emotions bubbled in the cauldron of his heart as he remembered the good times and the bad.

For many years I read this passage with an assumption firmly planted in my brain that kept me from seeing its most profound truth. I assumed that all of the times Solomon describes are separate moments in our lives. I assumed that we had to get through one before we could start the next, like chapters in a book or scenes from a movie. Take these lines, for example, which I think hold the secret to healthy aging: "A time to cry and a time to laugh. A time to grieve and a time to dance." Those sound like very different events, don't they? For example, a time to cry and grieve could be a funeral; a time to laugh and dance could be a wedding. Two separate experiences—one happy, one sad, and never the twain shall meet. Simple stuff.

But as I have gotten older, I've come to realize that it's *not* that simple, that the times of our lives can overlap, that a time to cry can also be a time to laugh and a time to grieve can also be a time to dance. Let me share a personal example.

If we ever meet, you'll notice I have an inch-and-a-half

scar high on my forehead. A couple of years ago, I noticed a red, itchy abrasion that wouldn't go away. The dime-size spot turned out to be skin cancer. The scar is my souvenir from the surgery. I got the cancer because I started losing my hair when I was in my twenties and wasn't smart enough to put on a hat when I played golf or went fishing, which I did all the time in those days. Now, for the rest of my life, I'm going to be making regular trips to the dermatologist. At some point I'll probably have to have my head sliced open again because, according to my doctor, it's not the sun I'm getting today but the sun I got thirty years ago that's doing this to me.

So I have a reason to grieve. I could just kick myself for being so thoughtless and not listening to the people who told me to wear a hat. I'm ashamed to say it, but I didn't want to acquire a golfer's tan—I was more concerned about that than I was about protecting my skin. It never once occurred to me that a golfer's tan wouldn't kill me but skin cancer could. Yes, I have a reason to grieve.

But at the same time, I have reasons to dance. My cancer is gone, I have a great doctor who gives me good care, I am much wiser than I used to be, and I have a perfect object lesson to use when I encourage people (especially young people) to take care of their skin. I simply point to my scar and say, "If you don't want one of these, better wear a hat or put on some sunscreen." It's amazing how a scar gets people's attention.

You see what I mean? The times of our lives often overlap.

If you're in your forties or fifties (or even older), I'm sure you can think of some reasons to grieve. You've probably got a few failures on your résumé. You've probably been run over a few times. I wouldn't be surprised if you have some dandy little scars of your own to point to. Just the fact that you'll never be young again, that you'll never have the energy you once had, or that you'll never again draw the stares of handsome young men could be a little depressing.

But you also have reasons to get out your dancing shoes.

For one thing, I'm guessing you feel much less pressure to look a certain way. You still care about your looks, but you don't obsess over them as you once did, because you're no longer out there trying to grab the attention of the next available hunk to come sauntering by. You no longer say dumb things like, "I'd give a year of my life for an inch off each thigh." Nor are you still trying to squeeze into jeans that are a size (or two) too small or buying shoes that kill your feet just because they're cute. Somewhere along the line it dawned on you that it's better to be comfortable. That was a huge, liberating breakthrough, wasn't it?

You're probably also enjoying your family more than you used to. Remember those days when everything you said to your teenagers drew a roll of the eyes and a theatrical sigh of exasperation? Remember when your son's bedroom bore all the marks of a toxic waste dump? Remember when your daughter brought home that boy with the dangly earrings, the crooked baseball cap three sizes too big, and six inches of boxer shorts showing? Be honest. Who did you want to kill more, them or yourself?

But now look at your kids. They seem practically normal. And wonder of wonders, they actually ask for your advice occasionally!

And what about those grandkids they gave you? As someone who became a grandpa for the first time a couple of years ago, I have to say this is the most fun I've ever had. Hearing her say "Papa!" in that little two-year-old voice when she walks into our house and seeing her run and jump into my arms is almost more joy than I can bear.

And be honest, aren't you also expanding your horizons as you get older? When we are young, we have tunnel vision. We listen to music because it's popular, never mind that it makes us cringe. We know all our friends are listening to it, so we listen to it too. Same thing with television shows and movies and even the friends we hang out with. But at some point, didn't you begin to realize that you'd been shortchanging yourself? Now you find yourself watching the Discovery Channel more and sitcoms less. You find yourself liking jazz or classical music or reading actual books instead of supermarket gossip rags. You take more of an interest in politics and current events. You've discovered the joys of golf or gardening or hiking or scrapbooking. You find yourself wanting to go someplace besides the beach on vacation. And you make friends with people simply because they're interesting and likable.

Honestly, I don't know a single woman who isn't more intriguing at fifty than she was at twenty-five.

And then there's sex.

Research shows that 87 percent of married men and 89 percent of married women between the ages of sixty and sixty-four are sexually active, and 25 percent of married people seventy-five and older have intercourse once a week. Even more thought provoking is the fact that 70 percent of people sixty and older say they are happier with their sex lives than they were when they were in their forties.[39]

How can this be? Probably because most of these people aren't working sixty or seventy hours a week and coming home dead tired. They aren't distracted by career pressures and interrupted by calls from the office. They aren't getting up in the middle of the night to feed babies. They don't have kids in the next bedroom who might overhear something. Most of all, they've mellowed, grown comfortable with each other, and they probably have fewer arguments.

Finally, I'm guessing that you're getting more spiritual as you get older. I see this all the time as a pastor. I'm constantly meeting people in their fifties (or older) who are experiencing a spiritual awakening. As younger people they were too busy or too preoccupied or even too arrogant to want anything to do with religion. But it's amazing how a heart condition or a chronic back ailment or the death of a parent starts putting thoughts of mortality into your head. Suddenly, you realize you're not going to live forever after all, and you start thinking about what comes next. I've found people who come to the Lord (or come *back* to the Lord) in their fifties and beyond to be some of the happiest and most energetic believers I've ever known. After a lifetime of denying their deepest need, they find that it feels wonderful to be meeting it.

You see how this works? Simply put, Solomon's secret to maintaining a so-much-more-than-sexy lifestyle through-out your life is to maintain good balance. For every reason to cry, find a reason to laugh. For every moment of grieving, find an excuse to jump up and dance a little jig. Don't think for one minute that life has to be an either-or proposition. Make up your mind that, come what may, you're going to maintain a great attitude toward life.

Solomon's Secret in Action

A special group of women have capitalized on this secret in a big way. They are the ladies of the Red Hat Society. They are some of the most vibrant and active retirees I've ever met.

I first encountered the Red Hatters a few years ago when my wife and I walked into a restaurant. The hostess seated us not far from a group of about a dozen older women who were dressed in the gaudiest garb I'd ever seen. There were hats of every shape and size (all of them red), feather boas (both red and purple), plus baubles, bangles, and beads.

But most of all, there was laughter—wild, rambunctious laughter.

At first I was a little annoyed. Why didn't those women pipe down? But the longer we sat there, the more I sensed that I was witnessing something wonderful. Those women were having the time of their lives. All of them were old enough to have experienced some real heartache. I would have bet the farm that all of them were either widowed, divorced, struggling financially, fighting health problems, or worried sick about prodigal sons or daughters. Yet no one else in the place was having as much fun as they were. Proverbs 17:22 says, "A cheerful heart is good medicine." That verse came to life before my very eyes.

Since then I have learned that the Red Hat Society is quite a big deal. Multiple chapters can be found in every state and many foreign countries. Sue Ellen Cooper, the society's founder, explains the bond its members share: "Our primary appeal is our determination to find the joy in life, to grasp the fun there is to be had at this age— fifty and beyond. We have been wives, mothers, and, often, career women. We are now in a different place in our lives. . . . Each of us knows that she probably has less time left than she has already experienced. Time is even more precious than before. None of us wants to squander any of it."[40]

Ms. Cooper also points out that doctors all over the country have written prescriptions advising their patients to join a chapter of the Red Hat Society. They see being a part of such an upbeat, active group as a way of counterbalancing the pressures, challenges, and disappointments that can cause aging women to feel disconnected and useless.

The point is, whether they know it or not, these women have tapped into the power of Ecclesiastes 3:4. They have looked for and found reasons to dance at a time when other women have found only reasons to grieve. If Solomon came back for a day and ran into a group of boisterous Red Hatters in a restaurant, I think he would point and say, "Now *that's* what I'm talkin' about!"

Solomon's Secret #2, The Secret of the Secret

But the chapter can't end here because there is another passage in Ecclesiastes that I believe takes us even deeper, down to the real heart of the matter. It's the secret of the secret, so to speak, two verses that explain what has to be in the heart of an aging woman before she will decide to put on an outrageous hat and party like a schoolgirl. The passage is Ecclesiastes 5:19, 20, which says, "To enjoy your work and accept your lot in life—this is indeed a gift from God. God keeps such people so busy enjoying life that they take no time to brood over the past."

And accept your lot in life . . .

Those six words are the secret of the secret, the real key to aging well as a so-much-more-than-sexy godly woman. You'll never be able to find reasons to laugh and dance as you advance in age until you learn to welcome and embrace every season of your life. The problem is that most of us have a hard time embracing *any* of the seasons of our lives. No matter where we are on life's journey, we seem to always be longing for another time.

There are millions of students who wish they were out of school, and millions of nonstudents who wish they could go back to school. There are millions of single people who would give anything to be married, and millions of married people who would give anything to be single. There are millions of childless couples who long to have children, and millions of heartbroken parents who wish they could get a parenting do-over. There are millions of working people who wish they could retire, and millions of bored retired people who wish they could go back to work. Solomon observed this tendency in people and understood that it's the ultimate joy thief. People who are always longing for a different season are never able to enjoy the one they happen to be in.

How are you doing in this regard?

If you're fifty or older, have you truly begun to accept the fact that you'll never be young again? Have you really let go of the past and decided to embrace your present and your future with enthusiasm? If you're not sure, answer these questions honestly:

- Are you still buying clothes and shoes for looks without considering how comfortable they are?
- Do you ever lie about your age?
- Do you wear your glasses only when you absolutely can't get by without them?
- Do you keep jeans in your closet that you can't squeeze into, because you're hoping to someday get back down to that size?
- Do you feel offended when a sales clerk asks if you qualify for the senior citizen's discount?
- Are you still wearing the same hairstyle you wore in your twenties?
- Did you enroll in the college-career Sunday school class in 1968—and you're still there?
- Have you recently researched cosmetic surgery, liposuction, or Botox on the Internet?
- Have you been thinking about getting a tattoo?
- Do you perk up and pay attention when an infomercial about the latest age-defying, wrinkle-removing skin treatment comes on?

Show me a fifty-plus woman who can answer most of those questions with a resounding no, and I'll show you a woman who's accepted her lot in life and is ready to go out and buy a big red hat and start having some fun.

And there's one more thing you dare not miss.

After talking about the importance of embracing whatever season of life you happen to be in, Solomon said,

"God keeps such people so busy enjoying life that they take no time to brood over the past." In other words, people who joyfully embrace the seasons of life tend to squeeze every good thing out of them. As a result, when you talk to them in their old age, they don't sit around and whine about bad breaks and missed opportunities. They don't relentlessly complain about their chronic aches and pains. Instead, they entertain you. They bend your ear for hours on end with wonderful stories. Haven't you known elderly people who were a blast to be around? Don't you want to become one?

~~~~~~~

Back in the 1970s our family watched *Little House on the Prairie*. The series was based on the stories of Laura Ingalls Wilder, played on the show by a young Melissa Gilbert. I knew that those stories were set in the 1800s, so you can imagine my surprise when I recently learned that Ms. Wilder was still alive when I was born. She died in 1957 at the age of ninety.

Laura Ingalls Wilder led a full and fascinating life. She did indeed grow up as a child of the prairie and later became a teacher, wife, and mother. She and her husband, Almanzo, faced many trials, including his paralysis as a result of diphtheria, a devastating fire that destroyed their home, and several years of severe drought that left them deeply in debt and physically ill. If anyone had a reason to be bitter, Ms. Wilder surely did. But I want you to read what she wrote in

1923, when she was fifty-six, the very time of life I've been focusing on in this chapter:

> Not long ago a friend said to me, "Growing old is the saddest thing in the world." Since then I have been thinking about growing old, trying to decide if I thought her right. But I cannot agree with her. True, we lose some things that we prize as time passes and acquire a few that we would prefer to be without. But we may gain infinitely more with the years than we lose in wisdom, character, and the sweetness of life.
>
> As to the ills of old age, it may be that those of the past were as bad but are dimmed by the distance. Though old age has gray hair and twinges of rheumatism, remember that childhood has freckles, tonsils, and the measles. . . .
>
> And thinking of these things, I have concluded that whether it is sad to grow old depends on how we face it, whether we are looking forward with confidence or backward with regret. Still, in any case, it takes courage to live long successfully, and they are brave who grow old with smiling faces.[41]

Ms. Ingalls, who *may* have been sexy but was *certainly* so much more, couldn't have known that almost a century in the future a man would come across her words and feel amazed at what a fitting end they provided for his book.

That you will "live long successfully"—not in man's eyes, but in God's—is my prayer for you.

So Much More Than Sexy

For women who choose to try to retain a youthful look as they grow older, do you feel there is a line that should not be crossed? Is everything in play, or are there some techniques that amount to going too far? Think of some of the women you've seen who were obviously not comfortable in their own skin. What gave them away?

If you are over forty, what are some things you could name that prove you are not living in denial of your chronological age? If you had to give up everything you've learned and everything you've gained, would you turn back the clock and relive your youth?

Ecclesiastes 5:19, 20 says, "To enjoy your work and accept your lot in life—this is indeed a gift from God. God keeps such people so busy enjoying life that they take no time to brood over the past." What is your lot in life right now? Are there factors that make it hard to accept? Are any of those factors within your power to change? What do you need to do to enjoy life more?

So Much More Than Sexy

A Letter from Mark

Dear Reader,

Thank you for spending time with me here on the printed page. If you're an old friend, welcome back. If you're a new reader of my work, I am grateful for the gift of your time and attention.

One of my favorite quotes about writing comes from a guy whose books I don't care for but who knows a little something about writing, Stephen King:

> You can approach the act of writing with nervousness, excitement, hopefulness, or even despair—the sense that you can never completely put on the page what's in your mind and heart. You can come to the act with your fists clenched and your eyes narrowed. . . . You can come to it because you want a girl to marry you or because you want to change the world. Come to it any way but lightly. Let me say it again: *you must not come lightly to the blank page.*[42]

This book may end up being loved or hated, praised or panned, a best seller or a white elephant in the publisher's warehouse, but there's one thing I will tell you for sure: I did not come lightly to the blank page.

The very idea of writing a book for women scared me.

Partly because I am not a woman but also because I have so much respect for you—I was afraid I might not be able to adequately communicate that while also saying some of the hard things I felt needed to be said. It will be up to you to decide the worth of this book, but know that, for me, it was a labor of love . . . for you and for Jesus.

If you'd like to share your thoughts about the so-much-more-than-sexy lifestyle, feel free. My address is still **MarkAtteberry@aol.com**.

In God's love,
Mark

~~~~~~

Other books by Mark Atteberry

Free Refill
The 10 Dumbest Things Christians Do
Walking with God on the Road You Never Wanted to Travel
The Caleb Quest
The Climb of Your Life
The Samson Syndrome

www.markatteberry.net

Notes

1. Gene Fowler, www.quoteworld.org.

2. Angela Thomas, *Do You Think I'm Beautiful?* (Nashville: Thomas Nelson, 2003), 50.

3. Ibid., 7.

4. Michelle Copeland, *Change Your Looks, Change Your Life: Quick Fixes and Cosmetic Surgery Solutions for Looking Younger, Feeling Healthier, and Living Better* (New York: Harper Resource, 2003), 3–4.

5. Holly Wagner, *God Chicks: Living Life as a 21st Century Woman* (Nashville: Thomas Nelson, 2003), 2–3.

6. Grace Dove, *Secrets About Guys (That Shouldn't Be Secret)* (Cincinnati: Standard Publishing, 2005), 22.

7. Stephen M. Miller, *Who's Who and Where's Where in the Bible* (Uhrichsville, OH: Barbour, 2004), 107.

8. Merrill C. Tenney, *The Zondervan Pictorial Encyclopedia of the Bible* (Grand Rapids, MI: Zondervan, 1982), 341.

9. Leslie Ludy, *Authentic Beauty: The Shaping of a Set-Apart Young Woman* (Colorado Springs: Multnomah Books, 2007), 112.

10. P. G. Wodehouse, www.thinkexist.com.

11. Arron Chambers, *Remember Who You Are: Unleashing the Power of an Identity-Driven Life* (Cincinnati: Standard Publishing, 2007), 78.

12. Hayley DiMarco, *Sexy Girls: How Hot Is Too Hot?* (Grand Rapids, MI: Revell Books, 2006), 49.

13. From the documentary *The Secret History of the Bra*, produced for the National Geographic Channel by Winton/duPont Films, written and produced by Anna Fitch, 2007.

14. Eve Marx, *Read My Hips: The Sexy Art of Flirtation* (Avon, MA: Polka Dot Press, 2005), 35.

15. From www.aboardcertifiedplasticsurgeonresource. com/plastic_surgery/statistics.html (accessed November 2, 2008).

16. From www.msnbc.msn.com/id/23807734/ (accessed November 2, 2008).

17. Natalie Angier, *Woman: An Intimate Geography* (New York: Houghton Mifflin, 1999), 133.

18. Maureen Dowd, *Are Men Necessary?: When Sexes Collide* (New York: Putnam, 2005), 57.

19. Barry Cadish, *Damn!: Reflections on Life's Biggest Regrets* (Kansas City, MO: Andrews McMeel, 2001), 27.

20. Reported by Maggie Fox, *Reuters*, posted on AOL Health, August 9, 2007.

21. D. Q. McInerny, *Being Logical: A Guide to Good Thinking* (New York: Random House, 2004), 3–4.

22. James Allen, *As a Man Thinketh* (Stamford, CT: Longmeadow Press, 1993), 15.

23. Pat Williams with Peggy Matthews Rose, *Read for Your Life: 11 Ways to Transform Your Life with Books* (Deerfield Beach, FL: Health Communications, 2007), 41.

24. John G. Miller, *QBQ! The Question Behind the Question: Practicing Personal Accountability in Business and Life* (New York: Putnam, 2001), 110.

25. From www.rollingstone.com/news/story/5934268/wild_thing/3 and www.latimes.com.

26. Kathleen Parker, *Save the Males: Why Men Matter, Why Women Should Care* (New York: Random House, 2008), 130–131.

27. Neil Clark Warren, *Finding the Love of Your Life* (Wheaton, IL: Tyndale, 1992), 60–61.

28. Susan·Shapiro Barash, *Tripping the Prom Queen* (New York: St. Martin's, 2006), 12–13.

29. From www.sissyfight.com (accessed November 2, 2008).

30. Leora Tanenbaum, *Catfight: Women and Competition* (New York: Seven Stories Press, 2002), 29.

31. Annie Chapman with Maureen Rank, *Smart Women Keep It Simple: Getting Free From the Unending Demands and Expectations on a Woman's Life* (Minneapolis: Bethany House, 1992), 140.

32. Associated Press, "Vehicle Safety News," www.vehicle-injuries.com (accessed December 17, 2008).

33. Sherry Argov, *Why Men Love Bitches: From Doormat to Dreamgirl—A Woman's Guide to Holding Her Own in a Relationship* (Avon, MA: Adams Media, 2004), xiii.

34. James Dobson, *Bringing Up Boys* (Wheaton, IL: Tyndale, 2001), 162.

35. Barbara and Allan Pease, *Why Men Don't Have a Clue and Women Always Need More Shoes: The Ultimate Guide to the Opposite Sex* (New York: Broadway Books, 2004), 5.

36. The information in this section was taken from www.people.com, www.foxnews.com, and www.wikipedia.org.

37. Gregory Baer, *Life: The Odds* (New York: Gotham Books, 2003).

38. Suzanne Somers, *The Sexy Years* (New York: Crown, 2004), 5.

39. David A. Lipschitz, *Breaking the Rules of Aging* (Washington, DC: Lifeline Press, 2002), 164–165.

40. Sue Ellen Cooper, *The Red Hat Society* (New York: Warner Books, 2004), 8.

41. Laura Ingalls Wilder, in the compiled work *Especially for a Woman* (Nashville: Nelson, 1994), 418–419.

42. Stephen King, *On Writing* (New York: Scribner, 2000), 146.